TIPS AND OTHER BRIGHT IDEAS

for Elementary School Libraries

Volume Three
Sherry York, Editor

Linworth Books

Professional Development Resources for
K-12 Library Media and Technology Specialists

Library of Congress Cataloging-in-Publication Data

Tips and other bright ideas for elementary school librarians. Volume 3/Sherry York, editor.
   p. cm.
Continues: Shoptalk, ideas for elementary school librarians & technology. 2nd ed. c2000.
Includes bibliographical references and index.
   ISBN 1-58683-211-5 (alk. paper)
1. Elementary school libraries – United States – Administration.
 I. York, Sherry, 1947- . II. Shoptalk, ideas for elementary school librarians & technology specialists.
Z675.S3T493 2006
025.1'978222--dc22

                        2005027533

Published by Linworth Publishing, Inc.
480 East Wilson Bridge road, Suite L
Worthington, Ohio 43085

Copyright ©2006 by Linworth Publishing, Inc.

All rights reserved. Reproduction of this book in whole or in parts is prohibited without permission of the publisher.

ISBN 1-58683-211-5

TABLE OF CONTENTS

Introduction 5

Section 1: Managing the Library 9
    Arrangement, Appearance, and Order 11
    Displays 22
    Bulletin Boards 32
    Supplies 36
    Equipment 38
    Acquisitions 42
    Processing Books and Materials 45

Section 2: Teaching Library Skills 49
    Parts of a Book 51
    Kinds of Books 53
    Dewey Decimal System 56
    Finding Books 58
    Research 60

Section 3: Working with Students 63
    Student behavior 65
    Checking Books and Materials 73
    Overdue and Lost Books 76

Section 4: Working with Teachers 81
    Attracting Teachers to the Library 83
    Promoting Library Materials 85
    Working Together 89
    Teaching Together 94

Section 5: Using Technology in the Library ... **101**
    Computers ... 103
    Printers and Printing ... 107
    Web Sites ... 108
    Searching the Internet ... 109
    Useful Library Applications ... 110
    Technology Training ... 113

Section 6: Promoting Reading ... **115**
    Storytimes, Booktalks, and More ... 117
    Displays and Bulletin Boards ... 122
    Reading Incentives ... 123
    Student Recommendations ... 125
    Special Events ... 128
    Special Tactics ... 131
    Utilizing Technology ... 136

Section 7: Building Positive Public Relations ... **137**
    Teachers and Staff ... 139
    Students ... 141
    Parents and Community ... 143
    Special Events ... 148
    Bulletin Boards and Displays ... 152

Section 8: Working with Helpers ... **153**
    Student Helpers ... 155
    Volunteers ... 157

Section 9: Managing Tips for the Librarian ... **161**

About the Editor ... **166**

INTRODUCTION

Much has changed in school libraries since 1994 when the first volume of *Shoptalk: Ideas for Elementary School Librarians* was published. Indeed, the world of the library media center is different from the world as it was in 1999 when volume two, *Shoptalk: Ideas for Elementary School Librarians & Technology Specialists,* was published.

Those earlier editions of *Shoptalk* were compiled from tips published in *Library Talk*. In January 2003, *Library Talk* and *The Book Report* combined to become *Library Media Connection,* and "Shoptalk" became "Tips." August 2006 marks the start of volume twenty-five of *LMC*. School librarians, library media specialists, or teacher librarians, regardless of their official designations or how members of the public refer to them, have been reading Linworth magazines, contributing tips, learning from one another, and sharing the wealth of their individual and combined knowledge and experience for twenty-five years!

During those years we have seen enormous changes in technology and in school libraries. Personal computers, networks, the World Wide Web, and on-line catalogs have become commonplace. However, much has not changed since 1994 and 1999. School library media specialists are, as always, an integral part of the educational program.

Elementary school librarians in 2006 are still responsible for the management of their libraries or media centers. Responsibilities inherent in the profession include working with a vast array of people, promoting reading and learning, and telling the world about our important work in a variety of ways.

We consider the arrangement and appearance of our facilities. We try to keep things in order. We are continually planning for, installing, updating, and replacing displays and bulletin boards to advertise our wares. Often we provide supplies and equipment to meet the needs of students and teachers in our schools.

Many of us are responsible for purchasing new and replacement books and media. Budgets are seldom generous enough for us to acquire all the things we want to provide. Sometimes we conceive ingenious ways to obtain more materials. In ideal situations, books and materials are processed for us, but many of us still process the materials in our libraries.

In this new century we teach library skills and work with teachers and staff while promoting reading and building positive public relations for the library media center. We use technology to do all these things and more on a daily basic. We have embraced technology and use technology to make our work more efficient, to teach students and teachers, to promote reading, and to build positive public relations. We have educated ourselves about computer technology, and we feel a responsibility to guide others in the judicious use of technology as a part of the research process.

With the advent of *No Child Left Behind* and tightened accountability, school librarians are, more than ever, aware of the need for teaching higher-level thinking, integrating curriculum, and working collaboratively with teachers. We train student helpers, work with volunteers, attend conferences and workshops, connect with parents and the public, and in a multitude of ways make valuable contributions to the education of our youth.

Twenty-first-century elementary school library media specialists work with students in the library to encourage students to take full advantage of the many resources we provide. In a working library, books and materials are constantly being checked in and out. Almost always there are overdue and lost books.

Dire predictions about the demise of books and libraries have not materialized. Better quality, more relevant books are being published, more children are being educated, and elementary school librarians continue to work ceaselessly to make literature and information available to our students.

Elementary school librarians are usually on the lookout for ways to do more and to do their multifaceted jobs more efficiently. The definition of "elementary school" varies from place to place, so the editor has included relevant tips from middle school librarians in this collection.

Tips in this book are categorized into nine sections:
- Managing the Library
- Teaching Library Skills
- Working with Students
- Working with Teachers
- Using Technology in the Library
- Promoting Reading
- Building Positive Public Relations
- Working with Helpers
- Managing Tips for the Librarian

We at Linworth hope that you will find many valuable and practical tips to make your job easier and your efforts more productive. We are grateful for your loyal readership and for the generosity of elementary school librarians who are always willing to share.

As you read these tips, you may say, "I do that" or "Yes, I've done that too." Perhaps these tips will give you ideas about other tips you might communicate to your fellow media specialists. We hope you will take a few minutes to write up a single tip or many tips and send them to *Library Media Connection*. With your help we will continue the collaborative tradition that makes school librarianship rewarding in all the ways that count the most!

SECTION 1:
MANAGING THE LIBRARY

School libraries are multi-use places. The school librarian is responsible for overseeing all physical aspects of the library media center. Decisions about the arrangement, appearance, and order of the library must contribute to the making of a functional, accessible, attractive, and comfortable space. Managing the library involves keeping the area organized and uncluttered. Because there are many individual items involved, maintaining order among library materials is important.

Providing interesting, intriguing displays and bulletin boards is usually a time-consuming responsibility of the elementary school library media specialist. Often librarians provide supplies for students. Some are responsible for checking audio-visual equipment to teachers. Many librarians are responsible for acquisition and processing of books and media.

This section of tips includes the following topics:

- Arrangement, Appearance, and Order
- Displays
- Bulletin Boards
- Supplies
- Equipment
- Acquisitions
- Processing Books and Materials

ARRANGEMENT,
APPEARANCE, AND ORDER

Assistive Student

To build up one of our students with cerebral palsy and to save myself time, I asked a student to borrow a wheel chair as part of his grade level project. He then tried to navigate our library and noted on a map areas that were difficult or impossible for him to negotiate. He tried out our tables, desks, counters, and the length of cord on our keyboards. Another student has been asked to label things in Braille. Encouraging students to be analytical and compassionate about assistive devices and accessibility issues has had great dividends for them and for the library. Plus we are now more prepared to be hospitable (and legal).

Sheryl Kindle Fullner, Nooksack Valley Middle School, Everson
Library Media Connection • March 2004 (Volume 22, Issue 6)

I Can See Clearly Now

When redesigning a library, be sure to angle all shelving so that you can see between the rows from the charge desk.

Ann Patterson, Lindsay Middle School, Hampton, Virginia
Library Talk • January/February 2002 (Volume 15, Issue 1)

No Peeking!

To create cozy reading areas within the larger space of the library media center, hang a juvenile shower curtain using clear monofilament line from the ceiling until the bottom of the curtain is near floor level. Put out a selection of books and other media that tie in with the subject. The curtains are often available at discount stores for under $5 and provide lots of vivid color with no effort. So far we have used a saltwater aquarium scene, frolicking unicorns, and racecars.

Sheryl Fullner, Nooksack Valley Middle School, Everson, Washington
Library Media Connection • October 2005 (Volume 24, Issue 2)

Window Seating

To bring seating up to required levels without taking up floor space or purchasing expensive tables, we put an 18-inch wide, laminate-covered plywood counter under our windows. It is supported with simple knee braces of two by four lumber. Twelve high stools attract students as does the sunlight in winter. The counters also face our bird feeding areas and feature used binoculars and birding books.

Sheryl Kindle Fullner, Nooksack Valley Middle School, Everson, Washington
Library Media Connection • August/September 2004 (Volume 23, Issue 1)

What's a Good Book?

For students who ask for "good books," create two favorites racks—one for grades 3-8 and the other for middle school students only. They're stocked with books that are proven favorites with the students. When asked for suggestions, we now steer students to the racks first.

Ellen Matthews, Shelburne (Vermont) Community School
Library Media Connection • August/September 2004 (Volume 23, Issue 1)

Encourage Independence— and Better Order on the Shelves

To make it much easier for students of all ages to independently find the books they want, provide visual and written shelf locators throughout the library. The locators, available from many library vendors, are plastic book supports that measure six inches high by 1-1/2 inches wide and that clip onto shelves. For each section, use a label providing the call number, description, and a picture of the type of books there. For example: 636.8, CATS, and a small, colorful picture of a cat. Use a scanner to reproduce pictures and format them to the needed size (about 1-1/2 inches square), then paste them onto word-processed labels and laminate them. To guarantee that they'll stay put, tape the labels to the locators instead of inserting them into the slot.

Sonya Christensen, Park Road Elementary School, Pittsford, New York
Library Talk • September/October 2002 (Volume 15, Issue 4)

Editor's Note: Be careful to avoid copyright infringement when scanning pictures.

Good Uses for the Card Catalog

No longer need your card catalog due to automation or paper record keeping of a previous librarian? Donate it to your custodian to use as a tool chest for nuts, nails, and screws or to your school's professional center to keep lesson ideas on index or the back of old catalog cards. Both will be happy for the donation, and you will have recycled a piece of your school's history to be used in a new way.

Geri Ellner, JHS 72, Jamaica, New York
Library Talk • January/February 2000 (Volume 13, Issue 1)

"New" Furniture

The modern industrial or loft look of stainless steel is very appealing but out of our budget range. Our school had several old steel desks with pink or pale green drawers. Stripping furniture obviously is not in our job description, but stripping flat-front metal furniture is a cinch with industrial-strength stripper. My desk drawers took less than an hour. Now with a bit of beeswax, the whole desk looks upscale!

Sheryl Kindle Fullner, Nooksack Valley Middle School, Everson, Washington
Library Media Connection • February 2006 (Volume 24, Issue 5)

Removing Permanent Marker

If students get permanent marker on the tables or someone accidentally uses a permanent marker on a dry erase board, you can remove it by taking a dry erase marker and running it over the permanent marks. Finish with a damp wet cloth. Works every time.

Joe Holmes, Weston, Florida
Library Media Connection • April/May 2006 (Volume 24, Issue 7)

High Visibility Signage

To create high visibility signage that blends in with library furnishings, type the sign in a large, clear font and then copy it onto a transparency. Signs should measure smaller than 3 inches high. Use four-inch clear library tape to attach the trimmed sign wherever it is needed. Use this method to indicate Dewey ranges on the ends of shelves and the contents of cabinets. Every year or so when the numbers may change, the signs easily peel off and any excess gumminess can be quickly removed with rubber cement thinner. This method allows the color of the furniture to show through and is far quicker, with more options, than a label maker.

Sheryl Fullner, Nooksack Valley Middle School, Everson, Washington
Library Media Connection • November/December 2005 (Volume 24, Issue 3)

Favorite Character Paint Sticks

Here's a fun way to help primary students find their favorite series books faster and easier. Get some paint stirring sticks from your local lumberyard or decorating store. Spray paint them bright colors. Attach a laminated picture of the series book character to one end. Put the sticks on the shelves in the middle of these series books. The sticks will make locating and shelving books easier plus they brighten up your picture book collection!

Joan Arth, Alexander Doniphan Elementary, Liberty, Missouri
Library Media Connection • March 2006 (Volume 24, Issue 6)

"Posting" Information about Your Book Fair

The posters that sell as part of the Book Fair are hot items. Many library media specialists display them inside the library media center; another idea is to tape them to the library media center windows facing out, so that kids see them as they walk around the building. This is an extra way to tantalize students to come into the library media center! I also use the posters as prizes throughout the year.

Laura Stiles, Cedar Valley Middle School, Austin, Texas
Library Media Connection • October 2005 (Volume 24, Issue 2)

Festive Paper and Pencil Holders

Each season or holiday decorate the library with appropriate items to create a festive atmosphere. Part of the decorations can include small, sturdy plastic cups with holiday imprints. These are purchased very inexpensively, no more than $1.00 for four. Placed by each computer workstation, they are very effective and decorative paper and pencil holders that add nicely to the seasonal themes. They are easy to store and to replace if necessary.

Janice Gumerman, Bingham 7th Grade Center, Independence, Missouri
Library Media Connection • November/December 2005 (Volume 24, Issue 3)

Right Tool for the Right Job

Purchase handheld appliances at garage sales and keep them in the back room of the LMC. A curling iron can be used for smoothing and refreshing all kinds of bows, ribbons, streamers, and flags. Purchase a travel iron for pressing creases out of banners and paper posters. A hair dryer is useful for speeding up the drying of paint on LMC projects and for drying cloth after a spill is cleaned up. And an electric drill is great for stirring paint. Having the right tool at hand for the job makes it easy to delegate that job. (And of course, with the exception of the drill, they can always be used for gussying up the Librarian, male or female.)

Sheryl Fullner, Nooksack Valley Middle School, Everson, Washington
Library Media Connection • November/December 2004 (Volume 23, Issue 3)

Check Out Our Banners

Modern newspapers don't fit into those ancient wooden newspaper spindles efficiently, so we have turned our aged spindles into display rods for cloth or rip-stop nylon banners. We drilled a slanted hole into a small piece of 2" x 4", which was screwed into the wall near our entry. The banners are often on sale after holidays, but the "poles" or rods seldom are. The spindles are also great for hanging promotional T-shirts and ethnic clothing.

Sheryl Kindle Fullner, Nooksack Valley Middle School, Everson, Washington
Library Media Connection • February 2006 (Volume 24, Issue 5)

Ceiling Sell

If your library media center wall space is at a premium, laminate book posters and attach them to the ceiling. The kids that wander around gazing up into space might get a great idea for a book to check out. It makes an otherwise boring white ceiling a mosaic of good titles to read!

Joan Arth, Alexander Doniphan Elementary, Liberty, Missouri
Library Media Connection • February 2006 (Volume 24, Issue 5)

Creative Uses for Book Jackets

My small library has limited storage space; book jackets were overflowing boxes and shelves. So I devised a space-saving solution. I laminate them and make them into puzzles or turn them into bookmarks. Students decorate lockers and cover textbooks with them. We use them also for author of the month and for creating borders and columns on walls.

Carol Kotsch, St. Elizabeth Ann Seton, Wichita, Kansas
Library Talk • November/December 2002 (Volume 15, Issue 5)

Tape It to the Limit

Students love to browse through the picture books and remove several from the shelves. In order to keep the books organized and still allow students the freedom to browse, the picture books are shelved according to strips of colored tape applied just above or below the spine labels. A different colored tape is used for every one, two, or three letters of the alphabet denoting the authors' last names. It just takes a few minutes and a little practice to teach students how to shelve the books. They merely need to match the tape color, and make sure the tape is showing when they replace the book on the shelf. They are eager to keep "their" library in order!

Sarah Davis, Ashland (New Hampshire) Elementary School
Library Media Connection • January 2005 (Volume 23, Issue 4)

Elementary Book Jackets

When book jackets are seriously worn, but the books are still intact, invite a class of students in to "adopt" the books. Each student reads one book and then creates a book jacket for it that is then put into a Mylar sleeve and attached. The students use font skills to create the title for the spine. Students are proud of this "recycling" project and often come to check on the status of their books. An older class can revisit and adopt books from early grades and actually read the refurbished books to younger students one on one.

Kathleen Bronkema, Nooksack Valley Elementary School, Everson, Washington
Library Media Connection • January 2004 (Volume 22, Issue 4)

"Bin" Looking for Me?

Put books that students are always looking for, such as Zoobooks®, state books, Babysitters Club, and Captain Underpants, on a table in bins. This way students can easily find the books, and shelving them is easy because they just go back in the bins.

Beth Morris-Wong, Hillview Crest Elementary, Hayward, California
Library Media Connection • February 2005 (Volume 23, Issue 5)

Space Savers

Keeping books in an elementary library in order is an ever-present challenge. We use a free resource to help us accomplish this, however. We call them "Space Savers," but they're just cleverly disguised (spray-painted) paint stirrers from the local hardware store. Unlike the commercially available models from the library supply houses, our version doesn't bend, break, or slip from view, because the sticks are sturdy and large enough to be clearly visible. If we see shelvers at a shelf without one, we need only to ask, "Did you forget something?" and they go straight to the octagonal box that holds the Space Savers to grab one.

Toni Buzzeo, Longfellow Elementary School, Portland, Maine
Library Media Connection • January 2003 (Volume 21, Issue 4)

Separating Fiction

When I automated our elementary school library seven years ago, I gave the fiction picture books a call number prefix of PIC and the fiction novels a prefix of FIC. Both sections are clearly labeled. Students are able to use the automated card catalog to quickly find their chosen book.

Lois Quinones, Frank Zeek Elementary School, Ukiah, California
Library Media Connection • November/December 2004 (Volume 23, Issue 3)

Key to Good Order

To help my students browse for books, I provide library keys. These are large keys that are made out of thin plywood and are colorfully decorated. The art teacher in my school had some of his students paint these decoratively. Now, the children come to the library, select keys, and browse. When they take books off the shelves, the children put keys in the books' places. This helps the children return the books to their proper places on the shelves. I decorated large coffee cans in which to keep the keys, and put the cans on top of the bookcases in the library.

Kristina Aaronson, Henniker (New Hampshire) Community School (K-8)
Library Media Connection • October 2003 (Volume 22, Issue 2)

Table Doily

If your LMC is the location for your school's hospitality (luncheons, teas, meetings, etc.), you can dress it up quickly for some of the more special occasions. Fold a yard and a half of colored butcher paper in quarters. Three quick wiggly scissor cuts (one to take out the center, one midway, and one around the outside edge) turn the paper into a giant doily for your tables. One centers each large double table. Visitors will comment on how festive it looks, and the cost in time and materials is negligible.

Sheryl Fullner, Nooksack Valley Middle School Everson, Washington
Library Media Connection • November/December 2003 (Volume 22, Issue 3)

Secondary Book Jackets

When book jackets are seriously worn, but the books are still intact, create a new jacket. Photocopy a 11 x 17-inch piece of black and white checked contact paper or a sheet of wrapping paper (so it can be used over and over). Large pieces of brightly colored paper can also be used for the base instead of the checkered copy. If any element of the old jacket is still in good condition, trim it to a rectangle and glue it on the checkered photocopy. Print the title for the spine.

Encase all these layers in a mylar jacket along with the barcode and spine label. The freshened books will circulate far more often. If students are handling this project, they may glue on their own review of the book as well. This technique is far more fun than a standard book report.

Sheryl Kindle Fullner, Nooksack Valley Middle School, Everson, Washington
Library Media Connection • January 2004 (Volume 22, Issue 4)

Boxing Day

To keep organized, use the boxes that copier paper comes in. Cover the side edge of the lid and box panel on one end so they will look attractive when stored. Store in them the decorative items, lesson materials, contest displays, and forms used for each month. Label a set for finger puppets, hand puppets, costumes and hats, reader's theater scripts, flannel board figures, and boxes for stories that have a lot of props, like *Anansi and the Moss-Covered Rock*. Put all items in a Word table that you can sort alphabetically and search using the "find" function.

Pat Miller, Austin Parkway School Library, Sugar Land, Texas
Library Media Connection • January 2004 (Volume 22, Issue 4)

Shelving Paperbacks

Paperbacks for older students—books with spines wide enough to read the titles—can be shelved along with the hardcover books. Some thin popular paperbacks for older students, such as the NHL and NFL albums of players, can also be given regular Dewey numbers and put right next to the hardcover hockey and football books. They will be found because they're so popular!

Paperback picture books with thin spines can be put into bins on the floor with their covers facing out. Students can leaf through them looking at the covers. Seeing the covers of the books will help younger children when choosing a book. You can put the bins under tables if you are short of space. The call number can reflect this special bin collection with a prefix of "PB" above the "E" for Easy.

 Joan Kimball, Formerly of Hart's Hill School, Whitesboro, New York
Library Talk • May/June 2000 (Volume 13, Issue 3)

Catalog Control

Set up a small table as a catalog order desk with plastic Princeton files lined up and labeled with the alphabet. As each catalog arrives it only takes a moment to compare it with its mates in the file and discard either a duplicate or the superseded issue. You do not need to keep the individual catalogs in exact order within the files because it is easy to spot sister catalogs by their spines.

 Sheryl Kindle Fullner, Nooksack Valley Middle School, Everson, Washington
Library Media Connection • October 2004 (Volume 23, Issue 2)

DISPLAYS

Talking Up New Books

Displaying a new or attractively covered book at the circulation desk with a large "ASK ME" bookmark protruding from its pages is a good way to talk it up to students. Just make sure staff know why it would make a good read or whose class project it supports. And be sure to have several of these under the counter; they may not stay long!

Mary Strazdas, Student, San Jose State University SLIS
Library Talk • January/February 2002 (Volume 15, Issue 1)

Poem in Your Pocket Day

In April, to celebrate National Poetry Month, have a "Poem in Your Pocket Day." Take brand new book pockets, write "Poem in Your Pocket Day" on the book pocket, and affix the pocket to colored tag board. Then decorate the area around the pocket and laminate the sign. After laminating, cut out the slit for the pocket. Each year, you can write the date of your "Poem in Your Pocket" day on a slip of brightly colored paper, laminate it, and insert it into the pocket. This way, you can have a new sign each year by only updating the event date slips AND you are able to use some of those supplies that might just be gathering dust!

Laura D'Amato, Thoreau Park Elementary, Parma (Ohio) City School District
Library Media Connection • April/May 2006 (Volume 24, Issue 7)

Book of the Month

In order to help students and teachers to become aware of the books in our library collection, I made a display called Book of the Month. I purchased a wooden painter's easel for about $15 and foam cork board. With Print Shop, I made a big sign that reads: "Book of the Month." A book with a short blurb is placed on the easel. A copy of the book cover is also placed on the easel if a student checks the book out. Students can check out the book for one week.

Sue Dwars, Andrean High School, Merrillville, Indiana
Library Talk • January/February 2000 (Volume 13, Issue 1)

Planning Ahead

During the last week of school I make a list of the books needed for the beginning of the next school year. I then play a game and have the students locate the books and pull them from the shelves. I clean them and have a nice display ready for the first staff meeting.

Cheryl Hartman, Dr. John Hole School, Centerville, Ohio
Library Media Connection • April/May 2005 (Volume 23, Issue 7)

Balloon Mania

If you get a large mylar balloon for the library, use a straw to completely deflate it when finished and store it flat with no wrinkles. Most local balloon purveyors will refill mylar for free or for less than a dollar. You can gradually build a library of balloons for all subjects. In your newsletter, encourage people to donate their mylar balloons. An eagle, Yoda, and a butterfly are our best ones so far.

Sheryl Fullner, Nooksack Valley Middle School, Everson, Washington
Library Media Connection • November/December 2004 (Volume 23, Issue 3)

Book Jacket Mural

Students can create murals to advertise "good reads" available in the LMC. Using book jackets, students choose those jackets that appeal to them and read the blurbs summarizing the stories on the inside of the covers. In small groups, they design an overall advertisement for the books they choose, using a billboard-like design to attract attention. Collaborate with the art teacher on this project to "spice up" monthly book displays and to encourage students to discover new titles in the library.

Connie Cleary, Edison Middle School, Green Bay, Wisconsin
Library Media Connection • November/December 2004 (Volume 23, Issue 3)

Poetry Corner

To celebrate Poetry Month in April, try emptying your magazine display stand, then moving it and your leisure furniture to a remote corner of the library media center. Fill the display with poetry books, local poetry contest fliers, and student-authored haiku poetry bookmarks. Get science or social studies teachers involved by having their students write a haiku on something they have studied this year. Students can come to this Poetry Corner during lunch or common time to read their original poetry and listen to other's poetry. Then, when May arrives, transform this corner into the Battle of the Books meeting area. Place all the new Battle of the Books titles in the magazine rack to promote a summer reading program. It becomes a place where students can read the covers and meet the present Battle of the Books team members to discuss the new titles for the coming year and ask each other questions.

Gay Ann Loesch, Sun Valley Middle, Indian Trail, North Carolina
Library Media Connection • March 2005 (Volume 23, Issue 6)

Celebrate Dewey!

Tired of dragging out the same sets of books for various holidays and curriculum emphases? Try using the ten major divisions of Dewey: one for each month of the school year beginning with 000 and ending with 999. A local dollar store may have some very large modern metal stand up frames. Using fancy fonts, fill each of three frames with info on the Dewey number of the month. The whole nine months' worth of fillers will be stored in each frame. Simply swap out the info with a fresh page from the back of the frame each month. Decorate the LMC door with a giant 100's or 200's, etc. cut out of bright repositionable contact paper.

Sheryl Fullner, Nooksack Valley Middle School, Everson, Washington
Library Media Connection • November/December 2004 (Volume 23, Issue 3)

Spotlighting Artists

We focus on our students' visual arts talent by showcasing an "Artist of the Week" throughout the school year. The art teacher chooses an outstanding creation from each week's work to display in the front windows of our library. She loaned me an easel for displaying paintings, drawings, etc., and we have a small table for sculpture. I add a note that provides the artist's name, the title of the work, and the medium in which it was created. During Monday morning announcements, we announce the name of that week's artist and the title of the chosen work. I make certificates for the students whose work is shown, thanking them for sharing their talent and making our library a more beautiful place. I put a "smiley"-face sticker on the certificate and present it to the students with a candy treat. To publicize our local talent, I wrote a brief article for our local newspaper describing the program and included a picture of several of the students whose work had been shown.

Julia Steger, Clifton Middle School, Covington, Virginia
Library Talk • September/October 2002 (Volume 15, Issue 4)

Stuffed Animals Decorations

Visit garage sales and/or Goodwill/Salvation Army stores to purchase book character puppets or dolls. They have great things for a fraction of the regular price. Once a year, I have a "Bring a stuffed animal to library day" where we try to find books in which the students' stuffed animals, dolls, or toys appear. The students enjoy it, they use research skills, and I have magically created a great display!

Roberta Z. Arguello, American Nicaraguan School, Managua, Nicaragua
Library Media Connection • November/December 2004 (Volume 23, Issue 3)

PROPer Display

A great way to get kids attention with a display is to have a "prop spot." Put a prop next to a book and the kids must read the book to figure out what the book has to do with the prop. Kids' interest and curiosity are piqued, and the book usually flies off the display within the same day that you put it up!

Tara Lockwood, Westmoor Elementary School, Northbrook, Illinois
Library Media Connection • April/May 2006 (Volume 24, Issue 7)

High Carb Reading

My book orders suddenly filled up with Bread books, and not the recipe kind: The Breadwinner; *The Bread Winner; Burned Bread and Chutney; The Risen Bread; The Bread Loaf* (poetry anthology); *Only Bread, Only Light; Peace! Land! Bread!; Peace and Bread;* and *White Bread Competition,* etc. In the past to showcase depression era books on breadlines such as those from the Dear America series, I borrowed several automatic breadmakers and purchased breadmix on sale. The wafting aroma lured some non-library users into my clutches. Sometimes librarians neglect the sense of smell in promoting media. Think of it as an olfactory bulletin board.

Sheryl Fullner, Nooksack Valley Middle School, Everson, Washington
Library Media Connection • March 2005 (Volume 23, Issue 6)

"Author of the Month"

Every month highlight a different author by displaying a matted picture and a brief biography. Below that, display a list of their published books and put copies of their books in colorful baskets. When the students come in, highlight the author and then read one of their books. The following month, move the display to another wall and highlight another author. By the end of the year there are about 10 authors with which the students are very familiar.

Patricia Perret Megerle, Ridgeview Elementary, San Antonio, Texas
Library Media Connection • November/December 2005 (Volume 24, Issue 3)

Uses for Old CDs

Catch students' eyes and attention by using old CD's for library media center decorations. Collect and save advertising and out-of-date CD's. Use "sticky tack"/ "gummy" to stick CD's directly on media center walls. Be sure to mount them with the shiny sides facing out. Rubber cement can be used to make CD's part of a bulletin board display. Use string to suspend CD's (back-to-back) from the library media center ceiling. Not only do the CD's get students' attention, they are also quick, easy, bright, and attractive.

Deb Logan, Taft Middle School, Marion, Ohio
Library Talk • September/October 2000 (Volume 13, Issue 4)

A Fishy Display Case

In our library media center we often display arts, crafts, and collections along with our books. Used upside down aquariums are crisp looking substitutes for expensive cases. They may often be purchased for less than five dollars at yard sales and thrift shops. They fit most standard library shelves and are easy to change by simply lifting one edge to insert new items.

Sheryl Fullner, Nooksack Valley Middle School Everson, Washington
Library Media Connection • November/December 2003 (Volume 22, Issue 3)

Return to Display

About two weeks before the end of each month, pull the seasonal books for the upcoming month. Put all items on reserve for a patron named "March LMC Display." Circulate the items as usual; however, when they are returned and scanned, they will cause an error message to appear. The message states that the item is "reserved for March LMC Display." Your volunteers will know exactly where to put the book—back on the monthly student display.

Beverly Frett, Robert Clow Elementary School, Naperville, Illinois
Library Media Connection • January 2006 (Volume 24, Issue 4)

Throw in the Towel

Pricey teen posters promoting reading are sometimes dull photographs accompanied by captions such as "Rockin' Good Read." Instead of posters, our library purchases end-of-the-season beach towels, which are frequently marked down to about $7.00—far cheaper, more durable, and considerably flashier when suspended from a dowel attached to our ceiling hooks with monofilament fishing line. They store without creasing and make great reading incentive prizes. Large print captions on paper can be stapled to them with a long bindery stapler.

Sheryl Kindle Fullner, Nooksack Valley Middle School, Everson, Washington
Library Media Connection • August/September 2004 (Volume 23, Issue 1)

Showcasing New Materials

Make sure that students have an opportunity to browse new book purchases. Since many children rarely receive a new book, they enjoy handling and looking at the new material. I display new books on a table. When classes come to the library, I take a few minutes to show the books and comment about books that are special. Often I use this time for a short booktalk to generate interest. Books remain on display for one week during scheduled class time until all students have had a chance to browse. Then they are available for checkout.

Norma Jones, Bessemer City (North Carolina) Middle School
Library Media Connection • March 2003 (Volume 21, Issue 6)

Helping Young Readers to Find Their Favorite Book Characters and Subjects

To help my young readers find their favorite books, I have decorated the library shelves with stuffed animals and dolls representing Caldecott winning books. We have Arthur and D. W., The Berenstain Bear Family, Junie B. Jones, and Franklin, to name just a few. In the nonfiction section I have a Humpty Dumpty, the Gingerbread Boy, an astronaut, a fireman, and many different stuffed animals. When the children ask for a certain book, I usually say one of two things: "Arthur can be found in the Easy B's under the Arthur doll" or "The dinosaurs are in the 567.9's under the dinosaur." All these characters make our library an interesting place to visit and help the children find books that they are seeking.

Mary K. Hobson, Vermillion Primary School, Maize, Kansas
Library Media Connection • February 2003 (Volume 21, Issue 5)

Clean Up Your Act, Clean Up Your World

If your library is often asked to feature student-created Ecology or Anti-Smoking, Anti-Drug posters, display these easily without making holes in your walls. String a clothesline from one side of the library to the other and hang the Clean Up posters with clothespins. Kids who have used dryers all their lives may be unfamiliar with fascinating pulley clotheslines. Retractable lines and pulley lines may be borrowed or purchased used. You can also use them to hang up photocopied pink and blue baby bloomers or baby pictures for school shower decorations. A hi-tech version of this (suitable for art) is available as a photo drying wire and clips.

Sheryl Kindle Fullner, Nooksack Valley Middle School, Everson, Washington
Library Media Connection • October 2004 (Volume 23, Issue 2)

Ethnic Decorations

Ethnic clothing is a great visual tie-in to library promotions. We have borrowed a sari, a hanbok, a kimono, a Mexican skirt and blouse, and a tribal button blanket to promote different holidays such as Cinco de Mayo and Lunar New Year as well as multicultural authors. To show garments off to best advantage, run a bamboo pole through the arms and use a ceiling suspension method. This way the display is not confined to a wall, but can be hung overhead anywhere in the library.

Sheryl Kindle Fullner, Nooksack Valley Middle School, Everson, Washington
Library Media Connection • October 2004 (Volume 23, Issue 2)

Going Mobile

Make mobiles from your antique, broken, or out-of-date a/v media. We painted old movie reels to use for a base, and hung a few film strips and their colorful plastic cases, some out-of-date periodical CDs, and a few defunct floppy discs. The middle support wire is a computer mouse (minus its rotator ball)! The students think they are great... and we find them to be entertaining and creative works of art!

Carol Bassett & Cheri Hansen, Arlington High School Library, Arlington, Washington
Library Talk • March/April 2002 (Volume 15, Issue 2)

Using Ads to "Sell" Books

Buy some clear plastic frames that stand up on their own (like easels) and in one of them put a recent full page-ad for a book or series you wish to promote. Put it on top of the fiction section where those books are shelved and stand or scatter several of the books near the framed ad. Those books will be checked out much more than before you displayed that ad!

 Julia Steger, Clifton Middle School, Covington, Virginia
Library Media Connection • February 2003 (Volume 21, Issue 5)

Pole Displays

In our LMC we use "barnacle" clips attached to our ceiling frets to suspend two loops of 24-inch clear monofilament fishing line. Through these loops we place a four-foot bamboo pole. This is used to support posters, etc. for library promotions. To reinforce different themes, we have substituted a red, white and blue dowel, a long golf club, a fishing rod, a broom, a mop, a long-handled butterfly net, a hoe, and a tree branch. The possibilities are endless.

 Sheryl Kindle Fullner, Nooksack Valley Middle School, Everson, Washington
Library Media Connection • October 2004 (Volume 23, Issue 2)

BULLETIN BOARDS

Yearlong Bulletin Board

At the beginning of the school year I put on my library bulletin board: "What books will we read this year?" For each month I have construction paper cutouts that pertain to that month. For example, apples and leaves for September, pumpkins for October, turkeys for November, etc. I write the title and author's name on the cutout for each book that I read to the students. This is a great way to recall which books I have read to the students. Also, it is nice because I don't have to change that bulletin board all year.

Marlene Luckadoo, Bloomingdale Elementary School, Ft. Wayne, Indiana
Library Media Connection • October 2004 (Volume 23, Issue 2)

Perpetual Library Bulletin Board

Set up a perpetual library bulletin board titled "Good News at My School" (substitute your school's name), and use it to feature newspaper clippings about students. Depending upon your locale and the time of year, the good-news board may feature sports, literary and community events, or other kinds of positive news about students. Give student library aides or helpers responsibility for cutting out or photocopying newspaper articles and periodically updating the board. This project contributes to a supportive, student-centered library environment, recognizes student achievements, encourages students to read, reinforces the analytical skills of the student library aides or helpers, takes care of the bulletin board, and makes you look good.

Sherry York, Ruidoso, New Mexico
Library Media Connection • January 2003 (Volume 21, Issue 4)

"Students & Teachers in the News" Bulletin Board

An easy, effective way to recognize your teachers and students who make the news in your hometown newspapers is to have a "Students & Teachers in the News" bulletin board. Cut out the articles and pictures and display them proudly on this board in the library media center. This has proven to be a popular attraction in our LMC!

Judean A. Unmuth-Shelley, Woodworth Middle School, Fond du Lac, Wisconsin
Library Media Connection • January 2005 (Volume 23, Issue 4)

Five Year Boards

I have two bulletin boards that I change with the seasons and holidays for my elementary students. Because the student population changes completely within a few years' time, I created boards for five years so that I can rotate them. After putting up the boards, I take digital pictures of them. I place a picture of each board on the outside of a large office envelope. When I take down the board, I place the lettering and any cutouts into the envelope. I will be able to re-create the board with a minimum of time, and I won't have to try and remember what it should look like.

Leslie Williams, California (Missouri) Elementary
Library Media Connection • April/May 2004 (Volume 22, Issue 7)

Mesmerizing Bulletin Board

We have a high interest bulletin board aimed at students ages 11 to 18. When some major long-term event hits the news and generates dozens of political cartoons, we post those on a low bulletin board at reading height. These cartoons are available within copyright laws from the Internet and only take a few minutes to print out five or six at a time. Occasionally the library offers a candy bar for the first person who can answer a trivia question about the cartoons. Winners' names are posted.

Sheryl Kindle Fullner, Nooksack Valley Middle School, Everson, Washington
Library Media Connection • March 2004 (Volume 22, Issue 6)

Student Book Recommendations

We let the students recommend books to one other in addition to the staff suggesting books to them. On a bulletin board beside the circulation desk in the library, students post ratings on the books they have read. As they bring the books back to the library, they can pick up a small form to fill out and place on the board. Each form has a place for the title, author, starred rating, and a "cliffhanger." (The students give a summary but are not allowed to tell how the book ends.) As students come in asking for book recommendations, they check the board to see what others think and choose books accordingly.

Amy Burkman, Keller ISD-Bluebonnet Elementary, Fort Worth, Texas
Library Media Connection • August/September 2003 (Volume 22, Issue 1)

A Poet Tree in the Library

No bulletin board has attracted so many visitors as our large paper tree whose branches were filled with student written poems. Poetry writing was the classroom activity of an English teacher who was thrilled that we highlighted her students' work. Of course, the students enjoyed sharing their efforts school wide. The state poet laureate who had evaluated their work came and awarded the local prizes in front of the library's Poet Tree.

Connie Quirk, G. S. Mickelson Middle School, Brookings, South Dakota
Library Media Connection • March 2005 (Volume 23, Issue 6)

It's a Knockout

Need an eye-catching bulletin board that promotes all of the many things you do? Try picking up various styles of socks at the local discount store. (I used baby socks, hunters' socks, athletic socks, Winnie-the-Pooh Socks, Dr. Seuss Socks, etc.) Hang them on the bulletin board. List your library's services (e.g., online resources, leisure reading, audio books, CD-ROM, etc.) on streamers, then position each streamer to come out of the opening of a sock. Underneath, add the caption, "Our library will knock your socks off!"

Christine Findlay, Centerville (Ohio) City Schools
Library Talk • March/April 2001 (Volume 14, Issue 2)

Other Uses for Book Jackets

So many new books now come with book jackets that have exactly the same information and illustrations printed on the front covers. Especially in junior and senior high, it is not always necessary to keep and attach a mylar jacket on a well-made book. Instead, process those books without their jackets and use the jackets for bulletin boards and other displays. You can staple the jackets on a bulletin board of "New Items" or a theme you have created. Students can see the jackets on display and then check out the book(s) that caught their interest.

Trisha Lake, Elk Island Public Schools, Sherwood Park, Alberta, Canada
Library Media Connection • January 2006 (Volume 24, Issue 4)

Fun Bulletin Boards

To integrate "fun stuff" with the library, in January for the Super Bowl, make a football field for your bulletin board. On each end are the two team's players. Use a die-cut of a football helmet of two different colors. In the middle of the "field" put in big letters "Tackle your favorite book" or "Read one of these winning titles." Each student who participates puts his or her favorite book on a die-cut helmet. The winning team gets an extra "fun" book for that week. It involves students and excites them to see which are the favorite books.

Lidia Vasquez, Wilson School, Dinuba, California
Library Media Connection • November/December 2005 (Volume 24, Issue 3)

SUPPLIES

Ordering Supplies

Our district orders most supplies from a large consortium. Instead of limiting myself to the library/stationery sections of the catalog, I use the whole book to order items such as eight-inch forceps (tweezers), individual alcohol towelettes, and a box of latex examination gloves. The tweezers are excellent for printer paper jams. The towelettes are great for sticky keyboards. The gloves will last through several years of student painting/decorating projects in the library. Small convenience items such as these, which might not get budget approval on an individual purchase order, are readily approved in this mass order.

Sheryl Kindle Fullner, Nooksack Valley Middle School, Everson, Washington
Library Media Connection • April/May 2004 (Volume 22, Issue 7)

Supplies on the Spot

I purchased a small plastic multidrawer organizer that I place on top of my desk. Students are free to borrow anything in any of the drawers. I have a drawer with pencils, another with highlighters, one with glue sticks, scissors, rubber bands, and correction fluid. On top of my counter, I keep a three-hole punch and a stapler handy as well. A bucket of crayons and a box of markers and colored pencils are also within easy reach. Rulers, which double as space savers for the younger set, are in a box nearby. Now I don't have to continuously jump up from what I am doing to go and get materials that students need to complete their projects.

Ann M. G. Gray, Pittsburg (New Hampshire) School Media Center
Library Media Connection • April/May 2005 (Volume 23, Issue 7)

The Shoe Bank

Students often ask to borrow non-media items from the library: a yardstick, scissors, a stapler, etc. Because I don't know each of our hundreds of students by name, I have them leave one shoe near my desk. When the items are returned, the students take back their shoe. Even the most forgetful student doesn't get on the bus with one shoe.

Sheryl Kindle Fullner, Nooksack Valley Middle School Library, Everson, Washington
Library Media Connection • April/May 2003 (Volume 21, Issue 7)

EQUIPMENT

Barcode Equipment Too

Track audiovisual equipment through the automated circulation system. Barcode and catalog all equipment and check it out using your system. If a piece of equipment is missing you can easily see who last checked it out. Use the automation software's report feature to run monthly statistics and see which items have been heavily used.

Jenni Seibel, DC Everest Middle School, Weston, Wisconsin
Library Media Connection • August/September 2004 (Volume 23, Issue 1)

Barcoding Library Equipment

I barcoded all our library's TVs, VCRs, and their respective remotes. Our barcode labels came with a smaller sticker with the same number. I put the small sticker on the remote and the barcode label on the VCR or TV. The TV and cart also each have their own barcode. When a teacher checks out a cart, TV, and VCR, I need to check out three items.

David Lininger, Hickory County R-1 Schools, Urbana, Missouri
Library Talk • September/October 2001 (Volume 14, Issue 4)

Control the Remotes

I put half of a Velcro strip on the bottom of our television remote controls and the other half on the bottom of the shelf holding the TV so that it's hardly visible when attached. This system really helps keep the remotes from "walking away."

Dawne Wheeler Reed, Hohokam Middle School, Tucson, Arizona
Library Talk • September/October 2001 (Volume 14, Issue 4)

VCR Troubleshooting Guide

If you are frequently called into the classroom to troubleshoot TV/VCR problems, try posting a troubleshooting guide on the VCR. We list the basics, such as "Check to make sure channel is set to 3," and "Check to make sure that the back of the VCR cable is connected to 'video out' on the VCR and to 'video in' on the back of the TV." The guide is laminated and then taped to the top of the VCR, where it is readily visible.

Jane Perry, Winslow Jr. High Library, St. Winslow, Maine
Library Talk • September/October 2001 (Volume 14, Issue 4)

Color-coded Cables

If you often check multiple pieces of AV or computer equipment out to the same teacher, to get the correct cords and cables with each piece of equipment, use colored electrical tape to mark all of the cords and cables that belong with one piece of equipment. For example: red for the VCRs, blue for the projectors, and so on. Then you can get the equipment returned with the correct cables and cords!

Jenni Seibel, DC Everest Middle School, Weston, Wisconsin
Library Media Connection • August/September 2004 (Volume 23, Issue 1)

Emergency Batteries

Keep some small (AA) batteries on hand for teacher emergencies. These are the size that fit small flashlights and some classroom games as well as various school cameras. Most disposable cameras come with a battery inside. We stop by our local film processors and ask for a bag of these used batteries for our library. There is usually lots of life left in them and they are free.

Sheryl Fullner, Nooksack Valley Middle School, Everson, Washington
Library Media Connection • January 2004 (Volume 22, Issue 4)

Smile!

For equipment with multiple pieces, take a digital photo of the item and all of the accessories that go with it. Using word processing software, import the photo and label all of the pieces. Include this guide in the bag or case with the equipment. Teachers can see what needs to be returned and check to make sure it is included. It helps the library staff also!

Jenni Seibel, D.C. Everest Middle School, Weston, Wisconsin
Library Media Connection • October 2004 (Volume 23, Issue 2)

Clip and Roll

The roll laminator you may have in the teachers' workroom tends to curl back on the rollers if one does not watch the document coming out. To alleviate this, attach spring clothespins to the two outer corners of the leading edge. The clothespins weigh down the plastic film just enough so that it does not curl.

Janice Gumerman, Bingham 7th Grade Center, Independence, Missouri
Library Media Connection • October 2003 (Volume 22, Issue 2)

Hair Ties

To keep all the assorted equipment cords neat and tidy, pull them together with hair ties. If you used rubber bands or twisties, the hair ties are easy to spot, don't break, and are stronger.

Barbara Schiefler, Alvarado Middle School Media Center, Union City, California
Library Media Connection • October 2003 (Volume 22, Issue 2)

Tangled Headphone Wires a Problem?

Headphone wires tangling and driving you crazy? Need a quicker fix than winding them up and putting a twist tie on them every time they're used?

Attach sticky back hooks to the side of each computer and hang the headphones on them. Variation: Tie up as much of the cord as possible with a twist tie leaving only enough cord to plug in the headphones and to reach the listener's ears. Leave one set by each computer. Put the headsets in self-sealing plastic bags.

Use rubber bands, which secure cords easier and quicker than twist ties.

Try these two items from the hardware store: A CableClamp® is an adjustable plastic clamp specifically designed to manage cables. The only problem is that five come in a package and only four of them are small enough. The other is quite a bit larger. The other item is a set of six "hobby spring clamps" made by Wolfcraft®. These are small plastic spring clamps just the right size to hold the wire together. Both of these items are quick and easy to use.

Renee Choe-Winter, South East Junior High School, ICCSD, Iowa
Library Media Connection • March 2003 (Volume 21, Issue 6)

ACQUISITIONS

Vendor Templates

Make a template with all the information needed for automated processing of your books and other media. When it comes time to place an order, customize the template with the specific vendor's address and submit it with your purchase order.

Aileen Kirkham, Rosehill Elementary School, Tomball, Texas
Library Media Connection • November/December 2004 (Volume 23, Issue 3)

Graphic Spirals

As the popularity of graphic novels increases, the bindings wear down and the pages fall out. A cheap way to increase the life of your graphic novels is to have them spiral-bound. This can be done at a local print shop or your school district's Print Services Department for about $1.50 per book—a small price to pay when you consider lengthening the life of the book by an extra year or so!

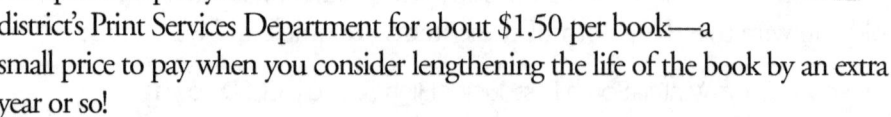

Laura Stiles, Cedar Valley Middle School, Austin, Texas
Library Media Connection • February 2006 (Volume 24, Issue 5)

Vendor Contacts

Whether by phone or e-mail, any time you contact a vendor regarding a purchase order, be sure to record the representative's name, date contacted, and discussion held. Attach a hard copy of the memo/e-mail to your purchase order so you have a point of reference if the problem continues. This is very helpful when the school district's purchasing department contacts you as to why the PO has not been closed out.

Aileen Kirkham, Rosehill Elementary School, Tomball, Texas
Library Media Connection • November/December 2004 (Volume 23, Issue 3)

Hot Laminating

Try hot laminating book jackets. Old books that are given new life are far more appealing to prospective readers. Laminated covers protect new books better than regular book jacket covers. Use a hot lamination process, and cut the laminate about two inches beyond the book cover at the top and bottom. Fold this extra laminate to the inside, and tape it in place. Attach to the book by strapping tape.

Ladonna Micko, Mickelson Middle School, Brookings, South Dakota
Library Media Connection • February 2004 (Volume 22, Issue 5)

Pam File

When filling out postcards or writing letters or e-mail to request information, flyers, pamphlets, posters, or other materials from agencies or organizations that send out such items, I always list my name as "Pam File." When the materials come in the mail addressed to that name, I know immediately that the item was requested specifically for my vertical or pamphlet file. It saves time: I can put those items in a pile to process all together at a later time.

Anna Hartle, Cincinnati (Ohio) Country Day School
Library Talk • May/June 2001 (Volume 14, Issue 3)

International News

Although our library is in a rural area, ethnic restaurants abound nearby. We encourage teachers to keep an eye out for any free foreign language newspapers displayed at restaurants. Depending on the cuisine, we have Spanish, Punjabi, and occasionally Japanese periodicals. We use these newspapers to give a world flavor to our magazine area without spending money. Plus they are a nice tool for making our immigrant students feel welcome and included.

Sheryl Kindle Fullner, Nooksack Valley Middle School, Everson, Washington
Library Media Connection • August/September 2004 (Volume 23, Issue 1)

Classroom or Media Center Scrapbook

Invite students to contribute artwork, book reviews, news reports, and other items of interest to a scrapbook. A regular scrapbook or something like a wallpaper sample book can be used to organize the contributions. Be sure each item is dated and contains the contributor's name.

Claudette Hegel, Bloomington, Minnesota
Library Media Connection • January 2003 (Volume 21, Issue 4)

Scholastic Book Club Points

In my school, the PTA runs the Scholastic Book Club. The teachers just distribute the forms and send the money to the office. The library gets the bonus points. With a recent catalog offering 20 times the usual bonus points, we earned more than 14,000 points on a $700 (school-wide) order. In addition to ordering books for the library, I use the points to order professional items, multiple copies of books for literature studies for the classrooms, classroom supplies (such as overhead coins or tangrams), book/tape sets, equipment (long-reach stapler, heavy duty 3 hole punch, and a cassette player), and lab packs of software. I've "purchased" (with points) an average of $3,500 worth of materials each year for the past three years.

Suzanne Weinheimer, South Mountain Elementary School Library,
    South Orange, New Jersey
Library Talk • November/December 2001 (Volume 14, Issue 5)

PROCESSING
BOOKS AND MATERIALS

Stamping Your Books

So you won't lose library materials that are returned to the public library and other district schools, invest in a stamp that includes all contact information for your library: name, address, and phone number. At least if a book is misplaced, the finder can contact you and you have a better chance of retrieving it.

Janice Gumerman, Bingham Middle School, Independence, Missouri
Library Media Connection • April/May 2006 (Volume 24, Issue 7)

Barcoding Videotapes

When processing videotapes, CDs, and DVDs, write the bar-code on the item itself, not just on the case in which it comes. This way, if a borrower loses the box, you can quickly determine the necessary information. You can check in the item and, if necessary, put it in a new box to circulate again.

Katie Sessler, Jackson Middle School Library, Grand Prairie, Texas
Library Media Connection • October 2003 (Volume 22, Issue 2)

Catalog Clips

When I do original cataloging, it is sometimes difficult to hold a book open to locate the pertinent information for the catalog record. To solve this problem, I use a large "chip clip" that easily clamps down the cover and first few pages to get to the information that I need. A large alligator clip would also work.

Janice Gumerman, Bingham 7th Grade Center, Independence, Missouri
Library Media Connection • August/September 2005 (Volume 24, Issue 1)

Processing Books

If you have a cart or a counter of books being processed, give each book a routing slip to keep track of what has been done and what needs to be done before it can be shelved. This allows any volunteer or student aide to keep busy. This is a sample of our slip which is printed on bright paper.

```
DO  DONE
☐   ☐    property stamp or label
☐   ☐    barcode attach
☐   ☐    mylar cover for jacket
☐   ☐    vinyl for paperback
☐   ☐    find in OPAC, add copy
☐   ☐    if not in OPAC, add record
☐   ☐    find Dewey in union cat
☐   ☐    make spine label
☐   ☐    attach spine label

Call # _____
```

Sheryl Kindle Fullner, Nooksack Valley Middle School, Everson, Washington
Library Media Connection • March 2004 (Volume 22, Issue 6)

Spine Label Bank

Some vendors provide extra spine labels. Separate them by "E," "FIC," and "B" and then alphabetize them by letter. Keep them in an old 3.5 floppy diskette box so they'll be at hand when a spine label needs replacing. This works well with Easy, Fiction, and Biography call numbers and is a quick and usable solution to fixing unreadable call numbers.

Lenore Piccoli, Mt. Pleasant Elementary School, Livingston, New Hampshire
Library Media Connection • April/May 2005 (Volume 23, Issue 7)

Swift Shelving

Even with an online cataloging provider, many free or reissued books that we receive are slow to make their way into the catalog. To provide a stopgap measure, we bookmarked our countywide library system catalog. We look for an identical or close match to the book in hand, pirate the Dewey number, and then add the first three letters of the author's last name instead of a Cutter number. This method lets us get the books onto the shelves swiftly. Because these entries are typed all in caps, it's easy to upgrade them to full cataloging in batches as information becomes available for download.

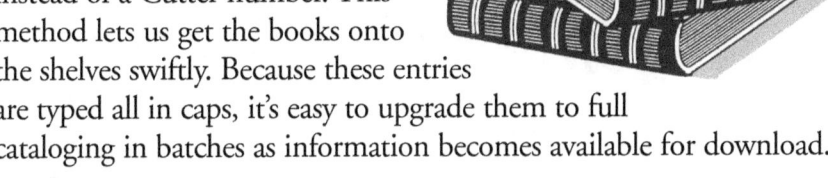

 Sheryl Kindle Fullner, Nooksack Valley Middle School, Everson, Washington
Library Talk • September/October 2002 (Volume 15, Issue 4)

SECTION 2:

TEACHING LIBRARY SKILLS

Effective library media specialists teach library skills in a multitude of ways, depending on the knowledge levels of the students involved. In the lower grades, students must learn the parts of a book, kinds of books, the Dewey Decimal System, and how to find books and materials on the shelves.

School librarians want their students to be comfortable in the school library setting, to be able to locate books and materials independently, and eventually to transfer that ability to other library settings. School librarians guide students so that they become adept at using library skills as the basis for life-long researching in and out of the library environment.

Tips in this section include:

- Parts of a Book
- Kinds of Books
- Dewey Decimal System
- Finding Books
- Research

PARTS
OF A BOOK

Computer Catalog License

In order to impress upon third graders how important it is to differentiate between subjects, titles, and authors when using the card catalog, I have them take a performance test showing how to enter this information appropriately in the computer. When they pass the test, they receive a computer catalog license that I make using the business card template of a desktop publishing program. I personalize the licenses with the students' names. Although third graders are usually anxious to learn to use the computer to find books, promising the "license" definitely adds to the excitement.

Marcia Dressel, Osceola Elementary and Intermediate Schools,
   Osceola, Wisconsin
Library Talk • May/June 2000 (Volume 13, Issue 3)

Rap It Up

This rap has helped our students memorize the association between call number and spine label. We use the couplets in a lesson on spotting call numbers. The students draw out the words call and spine as they say the rap.

> "These are the facts.
> I'll lay them on the table.
> Memorize them to the max.
> I know that you are able.
> The c-a-l-l number's
> on the s-p-i-n-e label.
> The c-a-l-l number's
> on the s-p-i-n-e label."

Sheryl Fullner, Nooksack Valley Middle School, Everson, Washington
Library Media Connection • February 2004 (Volume 22, Issue 5)

KINDS OF BOOKS

Genre Study

Here's a method you can use to begin in-depth study of genre with third and fourth graders. Give students a list of the various genres they will need to learn, along with definitions. After reviewing the list, read either complete books or passages (depending on length) representative of each genre. For each reading, students must first decide independently which genre they feel the material represents, and why. They then confer with other members of their group to try to reach consensus. Finally, students present all the choices and reasons, after which you identify and explain the best answer. For a twist, read passages that leave the genre unclear to see how students defend their varying answers.

 Norm Bagley, Cleveland (New York) Elementary School, Cleveland, New York
Library Talk • November/December 2001 (Volume 14, Issue 5)

Library Jeopardy

Make a large Jeopardy-style game board by taping page protectors to a solid colored shower curtain or liner. Use the bottom half of five protectors to hold the category title cards. Adhere pockets with clear tape, and insert cardstock on which you have printed the dollar amounts. Use a different color for each column. Hide the questions (or answers) behind each dollar card, and play with teams to review library skills, book genres, and plots.

 Pat Miller, Austin Parkway School Library, Sugar Land, Texas
Library Media Connection • February 2004 (Volume 22, Issue 5)

The Line Up

After book check, our students sit in the story area reading until dismissal time. Each week, I line them up by the kind of book they have. Even kindergarten has experts in fiction, non-fiction, and medal winners. Or have your five-year-olds show you the letter of the week on the cover of one of their books before they line up. Use specific genres with older students.

Pat Miller, Austin Parkway School Library, Sugar Land, Texas
Library Media Connection • January 2004 (Volume 22, Issue 4)

Magic Wand

When concluding a unit on folk tales and fairy tales have students create a magic wand with the call number that will lead them to these magical tales. Use a dowel, chopstick, or large straw and paste two stars at the top. On one side write 398.2 and on the other have students write their favorite tale and where it was from. It's fun and memorable.

Lenore Piccoli, Mt. Pleasant Elementary School Livingston, New Jersey
Library Media Connection • November/December 2003 (Volume 22, Issue 3)

Questions for Bookmarks

Our library, like most middle school libraries, was giving away lots of bookmarks. However, I noticed that many of them were forgotten in books, left lying around the library, or were sometimes destroyed. Because we were freely dispensing them and it seemed as though they were not appreciated, we decided to start charging for them. But we don't take cash; we give them out to students who are willing to answer questions about the library. Most students love the challenge, and we always give a bookmark, whether or not they know  the answer. If they don't know the answer, we prompt them or have them go around the library and find the answer. We ask questions such as "What is a biography?" "Where are the biographies?" "What is a call number?" and "In which Dewey section are the books about sports?" We have many more questions, and we try to match the question with the ability of the student. But we always make sure a student understands the answer and gets a bookmark as well. It's an enjoyable way for the students to learn about the library or reinforce what they already know. Some students come in begging for a question!

 Renee Mick, Franco Middle School, Presidio, Texas
Library Media Connection • April/May 2004 (Volume 22, Issue 7)

DEWEY DECIMAL SYSTEM

Dewey Stories

To make the Dewey Decimal System more relevant, I tell the origin of the system and then, dividing the 10 nonfiction areas into three parts, I spend three weeks reading interesting snippets from sample books. The children learn where to find these books in their own library and in any library, and they want to check them out immediately!

Lois Weems, Wildwood Elementary School, Sarcoxie, Missouri
Library Talk • September/October 2001 (Volume 14, Issue 4)

Check Out the 500s...700s...900s!

To make the Dewey Decimal system easier to understand and to create an interactive, hands-on project that all will enjoy, have elementary students work in groups and become detectives. Each group explores one Dewey section of the library and takes notes on all the different kinds of books found within that number range. Then as a group they design a colorful poster to advertise their section of the library. Students include drawings and words that convey what books they found in their area. Each group shares their posters with the class and then the posters are displayed in the library and the hallway outside the library for other students to use during the school year. This activity can vary in complexity depending on the age group but it works especially well with third to sixth graders.

Kristina Aaronson, Henniker (New Hampshire) Community School (K-8)
Library Media Connection • November/December 2003 (Volume 22, Issue 3)

Doing Dewey

Here's a fun way to teach the Dewey Decimal system. Since there are ten categories and ten school months, feature one group of one hundred numbers of the nonfiction section each month. On the board, write four or five "Facts of the Week" questions related to that month's featured section of books. First "booktalk" some nonfiction titles that are on display for the month, and sometimes break down the category into subcategories. For example, the 600s (Pure Sciences) have questions related to math ("What is a googol?"), astronomy ("Which is the planet closest to the Sun?"), paleontology ("Name the largest dinosaur"), and zoology ("What is a bustard?"). Discuss different sources to find the answers, then send volunteers to look in dictionaries, encyclopedias, almanacs, nonfiction books, other reference books, and lastly on the Internet. Students are amazed that they can find the answers faster in print than by using the computer! They love trying to guess the answers as soon as they walk into the library media center. Students make the connection between the Dewey Decimal numbers and the trivia questions.

Esther Peck, Wemrock Brook School, Manalapan, New Jersey
Library Media Connection • March 2005 (Volume 23, Issue 6)

Info to Grow

To help early primary students begin to explore information books without being completely overwhelmed by a large nonfiction section, select a few of the simpler nonfiction books from several high-interest subject areas and place colored dots just below the call number. House these books on an "Info to Grow" cart adjacent to the Picture Books. We keep them in Dewey order on the cart and have colorful number/picture labels on the cart shelves. The students really enjoy having easy access to these appealing nonfiction books.

Janie Schomberg, Leal Elementary School Library, Urbana, Illinois
Library Talk • May/June 2001 (Volume 14, Issue 3)

FINDING BOOKS

Alphabet Guides

To help students become more independent library users and find their own books in the library, make alphabet guides for students to pick up and carry to the fiction or easy/picture book sections to find the books in alphabetical order by author's last name. Make guides of the 26 letters of the alphabet, backed with construction or poster board and then laminate. About 20 to 25 inches long is a good range. Younger students use these in a library class or independently to help them visualize where their book might be on the shelf.

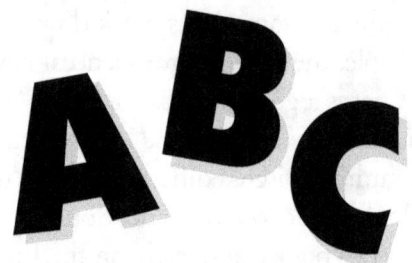

 Kristina Aaronson, Henniker (New Hampshire) Community School (K-8)
Library Media Connection • October 2004 (Volume 23, Issue 2)

Library Four Corners

Do your students still ask you where the fiction section is, or where to find a book when the catalog tells them it's at 398.2? This game gets students better acquainted with the library than library tours do.

To play, designate four places students can stand (the "corners") that are close to each of these sections: fiction, nonfiction, everybody, and reference. When you say "Go," students quickly move to the corner of their choice. After 10 seconds, say "Stop." Students still moving must go to the closest corner.

Then hold up a book that is obviously from one of those corners (take them from a box so nobody can see what's coming next), and have students identify the area in which it would be found. Students standing in that corner sit down.

Continue until only one student is left. That child gets to check out an extra book and/or gets to be the go/stop person for the next game. Involve the teacher by having her show the books and be the noise police—students who talk automatically have to sit down.

Pat Miller, Sue Creech Elementary, Katy, Texas
Library Media Connection • March 2006 (Volume 24, Issue 6)

More Uses for Book Jackets

Use a file of book jackets or pictures of books from displays to help students learn to use the catalog system and to find the books independently. After you model computer and shelf searches, students pick a book jacket and then look up the title/author/subject on the catalog system. They jot down the call number and go find the book (if showing available in the catalog) that matches the cover. Require fiction, easy fiction, and nonfiction searches. If a child wants to check out the book that day, take the book jacket out of the bin so that students can find books that are actually on the shelves.

Mary Louise Sanchez, Thornton, Colorado
Library Media Connection • March 2006 (Volume 24, Issue 6)

RESEARCH

Information Hunt

Using 3 x 5 cards, write the call number of a book on the top left corner of the card. Compose a question for children to research. When all have found answers, exchange facts found. Answers may be given orally or read from the book. Activity may be limited for concentrated study or without limits for a variety of facts.

Mary Agnita Coakley, RSM, South Amboy, New Jersey
Library Talk • January/February 2000 (Volume 13, Issue 1)

Carding RESEARCH

Create color-coded "fill-in-the-blank" bibliography cards (blue=book, yellow=Internet, pink=magazine, white=encyclopedia). Print three to a page on colored paper, cut them apart, and store them in a visible spot for students to use during research. Cut off the first row of a clear shoe bag (the kind with a hanger) and hang it on one of your reference shelves, stocked with cards. Students can use these to cite their sources while in the library media center. (Also share a copy with interested teachers so they can keep them in their classrooms.) Teachers can tell at a glance (from the color) which type of resources their students are using. Third and fourth graders simply attach the colored bibliography cards to their report or project. Fifth graders and up can be taught how to rewrite the information to make a bibliography page for reports or projects.

Julie Stephens, Calhoun (Georgia) Elementary School
Library Media Connection • March 2005 (Volume 23, Issue 6)

Teaching Bibliographic Citations

To help students understand what information needs to be included in a bibliographic citation, refer to the "Who, What, Where, When" concept. "Who" refers to the creator of the item being cited, "What" refers to the item's title, "Where" refers to where the item can be found (name of encyclopedia, periodical, etc. AND publisher information), and "When" refers to copyright date or date accessed. When you proofread a student's work, you can easily say, "You left out the 'Who' in this citation," and they'll understand. This strategy gives them some power to self-check their work and make sure the necessary components are included.

Laura D'Amato, Thoreau Park Elementary, Parma (Ohio) City School District
Library Media Connection • April/May 2006 (Volume 24, Issue 7)

Hunting for Citations

The concept of bibliographic citation can be difficult for students to understand. Try a reverse approach when introducing bibliographic formats so that students can experience firsthand the importance of correct, exact publication information. Hold a scavenger hunt. Hand out bibliographic citations to students and have them find treasures in a variety of resource materials (books, online or print encyclopedias, magazines, online databases, Web sites, or CD-ROMs).

Mary C. Jones, Eagleview Middle School, Colorado Springs, Colorado
Library Media Connection • February 2006 (Volume 24, Issue 5)

Animals Promote Research

To promote reading and researching using the 500s Dewey class, try a "Pet Show." Students can bring a stuffed animal for a research project. If you can, invite real animals to the library. The children will respond very well.

Madeleine Hoss, Metcalf Laboratory School, Illinois State University, Normal, Illinois
Library Talk • September/October 2001 (Volume 14, Issue 4)

Question of the Week

I post a question of the week outside the library door. Questions are diversified, so different reference materials must be used to answer each one. The questions may relate to the month, such as Black History month, or to a holiday, such as St. Patrick's Day. Students participate by writing the answer to the question, their name, and their teacher's name on an answer slip and dropping it into a box. Every Monday, the box is emptied and the answers checked. One name is drawn from the correct responses. This person wins a small prize. All of the correct answers are saved until the end of the month when one name is drawn to win a free paperback book.

Norma Uphold, Menallen Elementary School, Uniontown, Pennsylvania
Library Talk • November/December 2000 (Volume 13, Issue 5)

SECTION 3:
WORKING WITH STUDENTS

Elementary students may come to the library media center in classes or on their own. They may come before school, during lunch, after school, or during times when other students are also in the library. Although the days of absolute silence in school libraries are long gone, suitable student behavior is required. School librarians must be masters of crowd control while being friendly and helpful, not always an easy task.

Media specialists must deal effectively and efficiently with the checking in and out of books and materials to students. Inevitably, some books and materials are not returned in a timely manner and occasionally some are lost.

Encouraging respect for the library environment while keeping track of many individual items and maintaining a calm unruffled demeanor is indeed a challenge!

The following pages in this section contain tips on:
- Student Behavior
- Checking Books and Materials
- Overdue and Lost Books

STUDENT
BEHAVIOR

Gimme Five

A quick way to shape behavior of kids in the elementary school library is to use cue words and phrases. One that works well for me is "Gimme Five." When giving your orientation lesson at the beginning of the year, tell students that there are five behaviors you want them to exhibit when you hold up your hand, one for each finger. These can be such things as stop talking, listen, give me eye contact, put your pencil/pen/crayons down, put your hands in your lap, or other behaviors you desire. On each finger, I "tick off" one of the behaviors. I tell the students that when I hold up my hand from then on, I want them to do those five things, or "Gimme Five." Pretty soon, all I need to do to get the behavior I desire is just hold up my hand.

Donna Miller, Mesa County Valley School District 51, Grand Junction, Colorado
Library Talk • May/June 2001 (Volume 14, Issue 3)

Status Cards

Print out student names and barcodes on index cards, color-coded by grade level. Add a sticker to each card to help students find their cards when they are spread out for class check out, and laminate them. Use the backs of the cards to add stickers at those random times you reward them for returning books, participating in a lesson, bringing a book for the Book Drive, or some other reason. When the cards are face up, only the name and sticker show. The back of the card shows the stickers they have earned. I find that this rewards and motivates good behavior.

Pat Miller, Sue Creech Elementary, Katy, Texas
Library Media Connection • October 2005 (Volume 24, Issue 2)

Reading Jokes

When classes are waiting restlessly in line for their teachers to return, I grab a joke book and start reading. The kids quiet down, and my reluctant readers "discover" a book they want in the media center. This is an especially useful distraction during the holiday season.

Pamela Gelbmann, Madison Elementary School, White Bear Lake, Minnesota
Library Talk • November/December 2000 (Volume 13, Issue 5)

No Blame Game

To avoid "blame" type arguments, I use one magic phrase: "I am sure you did not do it, but could you fix it for me?" This applies to the group of guys with a purple pen sitting next to purple graffiti. It applies to the kid that I saw tossing the book up in the air and bringing it back with a torn cover. It works for helter-skelter chairs, litter, and encyclopedias shelved upside down. No arguments about who did it, just the necessity that someone be accountable for fixing it. No tool is fool proof, but this one has a high rate of success. Since it is not accompanied by an accusation, most kids seem to see this as "fair."

Sheryl Kindle Fullner, Nooksack Valley Middle School, Everson, Washington
Library Media Connection • April/May 2004 (Volume 22, Issue 7)

Hands Up to Quiet Down

Try this simple and effective technique to calm a noisy class. Say to them, "If you can hear me, raise your hand." One by one the students will raise their hands and stop talking. For younger students, move near a quiet child and say, "If you can hear me, clap once." Then move to another child. Pretty soon the noisy children quiet down.

Mary Ziller, Potter Thomas Elementary School, Philadelphia, Pennsylvania
Library Talk • March/April 2001 (Volume 14, Issue 2)

Look Them in the Eye

If you truly want a class to be quiet in the library, greet them at the door. Get eye contact with each child as they enter the center.

Ann Patterson, Lindsay Middle School, Hampton, Virginia
Library Talk • November/December 2001 (Volume 14, Issue 5)

Name That Student

I use index cards as library cards. When I need a student to open the treasure box, lead the line, answer a question, or take parts in a reader's theater, I simply draw names from the class stack. As students fulfill their special task, a sticker indicating the achievement is added to the card. This helps to spread around the attention and the special tasks and gives me opportunities to learn the students' names.

Pat Miller, Sue Creech Elementary, Katy ISD, Texas
Library Media Connection • November/December 2005 (Volume 24, Issue 3)

Faith in the Future

Some library patrons have a rocky, normal adolescence, but also seem to have great promise. When I see one of these students (alone, not with their entourage) I say sincerely, "When you are a successful businessperson, will you come back and donate a book to our library?" Of course I substitute whatever career seems likely: politician, artist, chef, or highway patrolperson. It's amazing what this vote of confidence does to melt and mend. It also says I believe in them in a way that a mere compliment about clothing, hair, or other attribute cannot.

Sheryl Kindle Fullner, Nooksack Valley Middle School, Everson, Washington
Library Media Connection • April/May 2005 (Volume 23, Issue 7)

Countdown

In order to help primary grade students get quiet and ready to line up after library media center class, play a book-related game. Read a counting book. Each table of students has a number. As they hear the number for their table, they line up. Students who are in line listen to the rest of the story. By the time you are finished with the book, you will have everyone's attention and the class is standing ready for their teacher to pick them up. There are so many wonderful counting books; it's a great way to share them. The same book can be used the whole week with all grade levels. Vary the game by reading the numbers in a mixed-up order.

Holly Cobb, Shady Lane School, Menomonee Falls, Wisconsin
Library Media Connection • August/September 2005 (Volume 24, Issue 1)

Library Access before School and during Lunch

I solved my problem of crowd control in the library by tying the privilege of off-hours access into our Accelerated Reader Program. Every nine weeks, I issue "High Point" passes to the top 30 AR readers in the school. This pass entitles them to free access to the library before school and during lunch. These passes are a major status symbol, and the kids who earn them are very proud of them. They use the computers, read, chat, play games, help me with tasks, and just generally hang out. Age and reading level don't seem to matter—this last period I gave passes to eight first graders.

Guusje Moore, Housman Elementary School, SBISD, Houston, Texas
Library Talk • November/December 2000 (Volume 13, Issue 5)

Quiet Reminder

Introduce a plush animal named "Whisper" to students. When students are becoming too loud in a classroom or media center, holding the toy aloft can be a reminder to keep voices low.

Claudette Hegel, Bloomington, Minnesota
Library Media Connection • February 2003 (Volume 21, Issue 5)

Passage to Field Trips

To keep track of students on a field trip, laminate a small number of "Field Trip Passes." To keep track of trips to the concession stand and the restroom, students who are old enough to leave the main activity with a buddy get a pass but MUST stay together. Each pass gone represented a group of 2-3 students. With a limited number of passes to distribute you have a better idea of how many are gone. When a pass comes back, another group of 2-3 can leave. You can easily identify students from your group by the passes they carry.

Janice Gumerman, Bingham Seventh Grade Center, Independence, Missouri
Library Media Connection • November/December 2003 (Volume 22, Issue 3)

Media Center Motto

To create a positive atmosphere for students, save time, and eliminate repeating directions numerous times a day throughout the year, I begin each class with a media center motto and end with poetry time. We have a yearly theme that connects to the library media center motto (reading slogan). Students say the motto at the beginning of every class; this is an active way for signaling they are ready for instruction. After the students say the motto they are expected to be seated, quiet, focused, and ready to learn. This eliminates repeating "sit down, get quiet, put your pencils down, and can I have your attention please." Some themes and mottoes we have used are: "Sherwood Forest"—the motto was "We Steal from TV Time and Give to Reading Time," "Oceans"—the motto was "Get Hooked Read a Book," "Western"—the motto was "Rope a Book to Read," "Africa"—the motto was "I Feel Grrreat When I'm Reading."

Mitzi Gligorea, Lakeview and Stocktrail Elementary School, Gillette, Wyoming
Library Media Connection • March 2003 (Volume 21, Issue 6)

Read Alouds

When classes come to the media center for book checkout, always read them the first chapter of a book. If they are looking for a particular genre (historical fiction, fantasy, mystery, etc.) then the read-aloud would be one of those. If they are in for a general checkout, find a title you have multiple copies of, but that hasn't moved much recently. Or read them one of the year's state reading program nominees. One chapter is enough to get the students hooked and yet allows enough time afterward for browsing and checkout.

Barbara Schiefler, Alvarado Middle School Media Center, Union City, California
Library Media Connection • November/December 2003 (Volume 22, Issue 3)

Poetry Time

To end class in a positive manner and expose students to a variety of poetry I end each class with "poetry time." Students understand when it is "poetry time" they need to: put away materials, push in chairs, line up quietly, and be a courteous listener. In grades one through six students take turns reading poems. I read to kindergarten. This is an enjoyable way to end class and eliminates students leaving the library media center with their last thoughts being the nagging librarian.

Mitzi Gligorea, Lakeview and Stocktrail Elementary School, Gillette, Wyoming
Library Media Connection • March 2003 (Volume 21, Issue 6)

Left for Library

We use clothespins as library passes. Each teacher receives three with their room number on it and a "landing pad." This is an L-shaped piece of posterboard that has "Miss Smith's Library Passes" on it. The flat part is stapled near their door, with the bottom of the L left free to attach the three "clips." When a student comes to the library, the clip is affixed to their left (Left for Library) sleeve. We can tell at a glance if the student has permission to be there, and passes are never left behind or lost.

Pat Miller, Austin Parkway School Library, Sugar Land, Texas
Library Media Connection • March 2004 (Volume 22, Issue 6)

The Before-School Library

Before school our students sit by grade-level lines in the cafeteria. Each morning about 20 minutes before the bell, a student comes to the library for an envelope containing 25 laminated library passes. She gives those to one of the duty teachers. Students wishing to use the library before school can get a pass and come to the library, where they read, do homework, or take Reading Counts quizzes until the first bell.

Pat Miller, Austin Parkway School Library, Sugar Land, Texas
Library Media Connection • January 2004 (Volume 22, Issue 4)

Never Can Say Goodbye

Tired of raising your voice as students rush out the door, leaving the library media center in a state of chaos? Try using music as a signal five minutes before the bell rings. Choose perky goodbye songs such as "So Long, Farewell" from *The Sound of Music* or an excerpt of "Go On and Kiss Him" by the Nylons. Delegate the job of clock watching to a student, and an orderly dismissal is in your future!

Deborah B. Ford, Instructional Media Center, San Diego, California
Library Media Connection • January 2006 (Volume 24, Issue 4)

Sponge Activities

Fun Activities to do while waiting for your classes to check-out books

Grades K-2:

- Play "Simon Says" Parts of the Book: Simon says touch the spine, Simon says touch the front cover of the book
- Sing "If you are happy and you know it" touch the cover, etc.

Grade 2 & Up:

- Read Poems
- Read Riddles. If the students guess, they win a sticker or a special bookmark...even better. Have the student read a riddle to the class. They love this!
- Read a new short picture book.
- Play "stump the librarian." A student names a fiction title, the librarian needs to guess the author. If the child "stumps the librarian" they win a chance to check out an extra library book.

Gayle Stein, Central Avenue School, Madison, New Jersey
Library Media Connection • October 2004 (Volume 23, Issue 2)

Devouring Literature

To learn kindergarteners' names quickly, elicit response to literature, and make attractive take-home projects, take individual photos of kids holding large name tags. Use the photos to learn students' names during the first few weeks of school. Make a simple, accordion-fold book, shaped like a worm, for each student. Have students make drawings after hearing stories. After several weeks, cut out the children's faces from the first-of-school photos. Glue each to the cover of a worm book. Glue student's drawings into its pages. Each "bookworm" has a record of stories "devoured."

Loann Scarpato, Abington Friends Schools, Jenkintown, Pennsylvania
Library Talk • January/February 2002 (Volume 15, Issue 1)

CHECKING
BOOKS AND MATERIALS

Boxes for Books

Label copy paper boxes with each teacher's name and room number. Each morning, student helpers whose classes will come to the library that day use the boxes to return their class's books. Books can be quietly checked in, renewal books left in boxes, and overdue lists printed before classes arrive.

Pat Miller, Walker Station School, Sugar Land, Texas
Library Talk • September/October 2001 (Volume 14, Issue 4)

Kindergarten Checkout

Checking out to kindergarten students is a tedious process because many of the students are unable to read their names. To help, on the first day the students come in, take digital pictures of each child and tape the picture to the back of their library cards. Instead of having to find their name at checkout time, they only have to find their picture. About six months into the school year, take the pictures off so their cards have names only. Explain how to look for their name on the card, and their skill of recognizing their name will develop quickly.

Paige Edwards, Barksdale Elementary School, Plano, Texas
Library Media Connection • October 2004 (Volume 23, Issue 2)

Check It Out!

To facilitate speedy checkout, we lay student library cards on a table next to a carpet runner. Students pick up their cards as they wait in line on the runner. Before they reach the counter, each child has stacked their books in a staggered pile so all the barcodes show and their card is on top. The books are easily scanned and the line moves quickly.

Pat Miller, Austin Parkway School Library, Sugar Land, Texas
Library Media Connection • March 2004 (Volume 22, Issue 6)

Get Carded!

Place your student library media center cards in either separate small manila envelopes or in an envelope by grade level if you don't have many sections of each grade. Pin the envelopes under a bulletin board close to your circulation area. When a class comes in for checkout, take down the envelope and lay out the cards. If using each envelope for a grade level, rubber-band the cards together by teacher's name. Students can easily select their cards and bring them up to the desk to be scanned. You can easily see who has not yet completed book checkout.

Susan Couture, Sullivan West Elementary School, Callicoon, New York
Library Media Connection • February 2006 (Volume 24, Issue 5)

Radio Flyers

My library is in a portable building at the farthest corner of the school campus. We purchased Radio Flyer wagons for students to use when returning books for a class. Everyone loves them. We use the wooden side panels to advertise upcoming events, etc.

Babette Longobardi, Helen Estock Elementary, Tustin, California
Library Talk • May/June 2001 (Volume 14, Issue 3)

A Recess from Confusion

For classes that have recess after library, I buy colored sentence strips and write each child's first and last name and room number. The students put the sentence strips in their books, and all the books are put in a basket or cart and go back to the classroom. After recess, the classroom teacher can easily distribute the books. The strips and carts come back to the library media center and go in a folder until the next week.

Beth Morris-Wong, Hillview Crest Elementary, Hayward, California
Library Media Connection • January 2005 (Volume 23, Issue 4)

Rechecking Books

Laminate 4" x 12" strips of construction paper that say "Recheck" on them. Leave 10 of them in each class book return tub. When classes return their books on library media center day, those wishing to recheck simply slip a recheck strip in the front of their book. After rechecking, return the books and slips to the tub, ready to be picked up when the class comes to visit the library media center.

Pat Miller, Sue Creech Elementary, Katy ISD, Texas
Library Media Connection • August/September 2005 (Volume 24, Issue 1)

Magazine Checkout

I check out magazines to 3rd-5th graders at my school. Students who have no other books checked out may borrow any magazine for 1 week. I keep handy large, clear snap-seal plastic bags with barcode stickers and labels attached inside the bag. When a child wants to borrow a magazine, I scan the barcode. When "uncataloged item" pops up in the automation system, I type in the title and issue of the magazine. Magazines must be returned in good condition in the same bag (so I can scan them back in).

Jennifer D. Burke, Centennial Place Elementary School, Atlanta, Georgia
Library Media Connection • April/May 2003 (Volume 21, Issue 7)

OVERDUE
AND LOST BOOKS

Saving Shelf

When students choose books to borrow, but have forgotten to return their books, no new ones can be borrowed. To help the students, we created a "Saving Shelf." Students who have forgotten their books can choose books during book selection time, and put them on the Saving Shelf for the next morning. Students know that the books placed on the Saving Shelf can only be taken by the student who put them there, and they respect that rule! The next morning, during a book exchange period before scheduled classes begin, the students simply come in, return the forgotten books, and take their new ones from the Saving Shelf.

Marie Mazzeo, Burnet Hill Elementary School, Livingston, New Jersey
Library Media Connection • October 2003 (Volume 22, Issue 2)

Overdue Lists

When sending out a list of students with overdue material within a specific classroom, I ask teachers to have students initial their names on the list and return the list to my box. I then put all the classroom lists in a binder. This helps to verify that students have been notified. On this first level of notification, before the individual notes go out, it helps to avoid excuses such as "my teacher never told me" or "I never saw my name on any list." Our school's discipline is based on documenting the number of contacts with the student. (It also alerts me as to which teachers actually do fall into the "never told me" category.)

Sheryl Kindle Fullner, Nooksack Valley Middle School, Everson, Washington
Library Media Connection • March 2005 (Volume 23, Issue 6)

Increase Circulation, Decrease Crying

When students come to the library with their class and have forgotten library books they need to return, have them go ahead and look for books. Then when it is time to check out, "save" these books on a shelf behind the circulation desk and give the student a "pretend" book to take home as a reminder. You can make a "pretend" book out of a piece of corrugated cardboard about the size of a picture book (8" x 10") with the following message: "Please return your library books and this reminder." The students take the pretend book home in their backpacks where it is very easy for parents to see it. The next day (whenever it is convenient for the teacher), the students return, put the cardboard in the basket on the desk, and "trade" the books that were at home for the books that you saved for them. Our custodians provide the cardboard from the many boxes they have to recycle and even cut them up for us.

Sonya Christensen, Park Road Elementary School, Pittsford, New York
Library Talk • November/December 2002 (Volume 15, Issue 5)

Round Up Misplaced Books

To help find books that students have checked out and misplaced, make a wanted poster telling the students that the following books have "escaped the library." Offer a reward for their return. List the titles and call numbers of the "escaped" books. The students who checked the books out are still responsible for them, but usually those students are the ones who later find the books. (You may not want to give a reward to the student who originally misplaced the book!).

Judy Wolbert, North Clarion (Pennsylvania) Elementary
Library Talk • May/June 2002 (Volume 15, Issue 3)

Year-End Fines

If you have problems collecting fines at the end of the school, purchase a boxful of candy from the local dollar store. For every patron who has no fines or overdue books when they turn in all their books, allow them to choose a piece of candy from the candy box. Many will pay for fines and lost books just to get a penny piece of candy in front of their peers.

Julia Phillips, Ashville (Alabama) Middle School
Library Media Connection • April/May 2006 (Volume 24, Issue 7)

Incentives for Book Returns

Nothing motivates children to return overdue library books more than a contest. Seasonal contests will bring back library books.
This really works!

> **During Christmas**—"Guess the Candy Canes in the Jar" or Red and Green M & M's.
>
> **During Valentine's Day**—"Guess the Candy Hearts in the Jar."
>
> **During Easter**—"Guess the Jelly Beans in the Jar."
>
> **Anytime**—Guess the chocolate kisses in the jar. Guess the pages of this book. (Use a large dictionary, not listed in your catalog.)

Gayle Stein, Central Avenue School, Madison, New Jersey
Library Media Connection • November/December 2004 (Volume 23, Issue 3)

Promptness Pays

To encourage students to bring back their books on time, start a promotion for the "10,000th Checkout" in your library media center.

At the start of school, set the circulation counter to zero and watch the checkout number increase daily. When it approaches 9,800 checkouts, make a morning announcement stating that whoever checks out the 10,000th book will win a bag full of prizes. Remind the students to bring their books back on time so that they may be the 10,000th checkout. When you have a winner, ring a bell and give the student prizes such as books, pencils, bookmarks, and other freebies that you pick up at conventions. At the end-of-day announcements, read the winner's name, along with the list of prizes. Then remind students to keep on returning their books on time so that they may be the lucky winner of the 20,000th Checkout.

Esther Peck, Wemrock Brook School, Manalapan, New Jersey
Library Media Connection • January 2005 (Volume 23, Issue 4)

SECTION 4:

WORKING WITH TEACHERS

Working with teachers is an essential part of the work of the elementary library media specialist. Elementary school librarians facilitate collaboration with teachers in a multitude of ways. They actively plan to attract teachers to the library and continually promote library materials to teachers in a variety of creative ways. Always aware that the library collection must be relevant to the curricula of the school, the elementary school librarian works with teachers in planning library activities that incorporate library use and research skills into meaningful lessons. In addition, the effective media specialist frequently teaches as well.

Tips in this section are:

- Attracting Teachers to the Library
- Promoting Library Materials
- Working Together
- Teaching Together

ATTRACTING
TEACHERS TO THE LIBRARY

Spoiling Teachers

Any teacher or volunteer who has a minor emergency heads for the library media center. We are fortunate to have an adult bathroom in our library media center. I keep it stocked with an SOS basket that contains hair spray, lotion, breath mints, sewing kit, simple first aid kit, safety pins, clear nail polish, hem tape, lint brush, and deodorant spray. We keep feminine items under the table skirt. Chocolate, tea bags, and cocoa mix are kept in the office. The goodwill generated by our dollar store purchases is well worth the expenditure.

Pat Miller, Sue Creech Elementary, Katy ISD, Texas
Library Media Connection • January 2006 (Volume 24, Issue 4)

Meet the New Books Party

Introduce your new books each year (and promote the library) with a staff "Tea and Chocolate" after school near the beginning of the year. Divide all the new books into subject areas and display them invitingly. Then have a goodies table with a fancy punch and platters of fruit and rich chocolate. The teachers will be impressed that you fussed so much for them—and that you are buying for their specific curricula!

Ellen Bell, Amador Valley High School, Pleasanton, California
Library Talk • May/June 2002 (Volume 15, Issue 3)

Teacher Feature

To get to know the teachers, create a "Teacher Feature." At the beginning of the year, ask the teachers and staff (including the principal) to sign up and each week feature a different teacher with pictures from youth until present. Make sure to have their favorite book "then" and "now" in the middle of the poster.

Tara Lockwood, Westmoor Elementary School, Northbrook, Illinois
Library Media Connection • April/May 2006 (Volume 24, Issue 7)

Reaching Student Teachers

Looking for a way to connect with new student teachers? I like to give personalized invitations to student teachers. I invite them to the media center for a tour of the facility, show them how to search the OPAC, highlight our district library media center Web site, and spend a few minutes showing them how to use our online databases. I also explain about some of the other services our media center offers. I provide printed copies of the media center Web site homepage and information with user names and passwords for home access to the databases. I ask the student teachers right off the bat if there's anything I can do to help them, and I check periodically throughout their time in the building to touch base with them. It's been a big success.

Laura D'Amato, Thoreau Park Elementary, Renwood Elementary, Parma, Ohio
Library Media Connection • March 2006 (Volume 24, Issue 6)

PROMOTING
LIBRARY MATERIALS

Compliments of...

Make a rubber stamp entitled Compliments of (Fill in your media center name.). Each time you find an article, poster, magazine issue, etc. that you want to pass along to a colleague, rubber stamp a post-it onto the cover and put it in his or her box. This way he or she remembers who passed along the goodies!

Barbara Schiefler, Alvarado Middle School Media Center, Union City, California
Library Media Connection • October 2003 (Volume 22, Issue 2)

Special Lunch Displays

If your school has special lunches for faculty (birthday lunch, holiday potluck, etc.), you have a terrific opportunity to display new library materials. For a recent lunch, I sent invitations to faculty members asking them to come to a "book preview." The preview time started 15 minutes before the special lunch and ended 15 minutes after. Books and videos were displayed on tables in a supply room across from the faculty lounge. The proximity of the display area to the luncheon was a key component of the preview. Teachers were able to browse (and check out) the new books at their leisure. This preview time was more successful than others held before or during faculty meetings.

Laura D'Amato, Lake Ridge Academy, North Ridgeville, Ohio
Library Media Connection • February 2003 (Volume 21, Issue 5)

Boost Your Professional Library

To boost your professional library, announce your new arrivals. While cataloging, create an annotated list of the new professional books, take a digital picture of the new books on the shelf, and send the list and photo to the entire staff in an e-mail. The teachers can read the list and description of each new book before they come to the library and know which books they are interested in beforehand. Teachers can even e-mail you and ask you to hold a certain book on the list for them! You might also add the photo and list to your media center link on the school's Web site, making the list available permanently for reference.

Ellen Proefrock, Lafayette-Winona Middle School, Norfolk, Virginia
Library Media Connection • April/May 2006 (Volume 24, Issue 7)

Spread the Word

Need to spread the word and get your co-workers' attention? Post staff messages over the school's photocopier machines, on the wall behind shared phones, in the bathroom, and by teacher's mailboxes. If you have a flexible schedule, these locations are also effective places to post a copy.

Deb Logan, Taft Middle School, Marion, Ohio
Library Talk • May/June 2001 (Volume 14, Issue 3)

The In"stall"ment Plan

To keep teachers apprised of new books in the library, turn bathroom stall doors into billboards. Use double-stick tape to affix a clear plastic protector into which you can slip a colorful book jacket with a brief annotation. Change them often. I call them Book Blurbs: The In"stall"ment Plan.

Kathy Parker, Ira Murphy Elementary School, Peoria, Arizona
Library Media Connection • August/September 2004 (Volume 23, Issue 1)

All Together Now . . .

One way to keep teachers organized with information from the media center is to provide them with a small three-ring binder. The binder contains any information relevant to the media center. Start the binder with information regarding general media center policies as well as a list of Web addresses for online database subscriptions, passwords, and the address to the media center homepage. Throughout the year, when you distribute important information in the form of paper memos, hole-punch the paper before distributing it so teachers can quickly file it. Teachers can also print out information you send via e-mail and keep it handy in the binder. If you are unable to provide each teacher with a binder, create a media center section in the building-level faculty handbook.

Laura D'Amato, Thoreau Park Elementary, Parma (Ohio) City School District
Library Media Connection • April/May 2005 (Volume 23, Issue 7)

Connect Kids and Library Resources

Do you have good fiction and nonfiction books that sit on your shelves unnoticed? Select one teacher from each grade level and ask them for display space in their classrooms. Hang book covers on their bulletin boards or put the books in their window cases. Put math books in the math rooms, art and music titles in the fine arts rooms. The busy teachers will rejoice that you are taking over one of their many tasks and most will gladly send a student down to the library to check out the books. Students will see what resources are available in the library to support their projects and assignments and teachers will learn about them too!

Dr. R. J. (Becky) Pasco, University of Nebraska at Omaha
Library Talk • May/June 2002 (Volume 15, Issue 3)

Library Research Tidbits

When sending out communications such as new book lists to teachers, I put a small bulb at the bottom that describes current school library research findings. This helps to promote the use of the library in the teaching and learning process among classroom teachers. For example, one item might read: "Current research findings have revealed that student academic achievement is increased when collaborative planning between the classroom teacher and the school librarian occurs."

Patricia L. Kolencik, North Clarion High School Library, Tionesta, Pennsylvania
Library Talk • January/February 2001 (Volume 14, Issue 1)

Forward Helpful Links

I subscribe to Refdesk Link of the Day at http://www.refdesk.com. When I receive links that are of interest to a particular teaching department or group of teachers, I forward the link to those teachers. It's an easy way to keep the library visible and helpful.

Ellen Goldfinch, Peter Holt Memorial Library, Bishop's College School, Lennoxville, Quebec, Canada
Library Talk • May/June 2002 (Volume 15, Issue 3)

Dream Grant

To convince teachers to take the time to suggest materials they would like for the library, print an official-looking personalized document stating that each has been awarded a $150 Dream Grant for the purchase of library materials for the school library. All they have to do is list the items they wish to have purchased or instead, just the subject matter. When the books arrive, make certain that each teacher receives "his" stack of books to look over before they are added to the library.

Sheryl Kindle Fullner, Nooksack Valley Middle School, Everson, Washington
Library Media Connection • October 2004 (Volume 23, Issue 2)

WORKING
TOGETHER

After Hours Check Out

Teachers wanting materials before or after the library media center is open would often forget to jot down their barcode numbers, so books "walked." Now we ask teachers to simply leave their stack of materials on the counter with a form that has their name and room number on it. I check out and deliver the materials first thing each morning. Teachers feel confident they will have what they need for instruction, so they remember to stack and wait, not get and take!

Pat Miller, Sue Creech Elementary, Katy ISD, Texas
Library Media Connection • August/September 2005 (Volume 24, Issue 1)

Teacher Book Display

Include a binder, filled with sheets divided up into 15-minute blocks, in your teacher book display. Each sheet also has a place for the teacher's name and the title of the book. The sheets are generic enough to be dated as needed. When a teacher plans to use one of these favorite books for a lesson, he or she signs it out that morning, whether it is for 15 minutes or hours. When the teacher is finished, the book is returned directly to the display. This practice prevents the teacher who is always early in selecting materials from checking out all the best seasonal books for his or her classroom and leaving none for the other teachers to use. This same display can also be used for special-event materials and seasonal videos and DVDs.

Beverly Frett, Robert Clow Elementary School, Naperville, Illinois
Library Media Connection • February 2006 (Volume 24, Issue 5)

Planning Forms for Collaboration

We all know the value of collaborating with teachers. But it's also important to know that much of the school library literature recommends the use of a planning form to ensure success in collaboration. A form allows you to efficiently record goals, decisions, and responsibilities during your planning sessions with teachers. The best planning forms are simple and straightforward, yet comprehensive enough to ensure that unit responsibilities, outcomes, and resources are clear and that the unit is easily replicable. In addition to taking notes during collaboration meetings, I take on the role of "unit-publisher": I write up a rough draft of the unit and distribute it to all team members for comment and refinement. I then "publish" our final unit document for all of us to use.

Toni Buzzeo, Longfellow School, Portland, Maine
Library Media Connection • August/September 2003 (Volume 22, Issue 1)

Reporting Collaboration

In order for us to succeed in employing the collaborative model in our school library media centers, our principals must be regularly informed about collaborative planning and library media center usage. There are many options for this communication, but I find the most effective vehicle to be a monthly report which summarizes not only the month's statistics, collection development work, facility and staffing changes (including volunteer time), and technology issues, but also focuses on the collaborative projects planned, implemented, or ongoing during that month. This gives me a chance to keep my collaborative work front and center in my administrator's mind. And whenever a fabulous collaborative project is underway in the library media center or a wonderful program is scheduled, I give her a verbal heads-up and ask her to stop in. This helps to garner the administrative support that collaboration requires.

Toni Buzzeo, Longfellow Elementary School, Portland, Maine
Library Media Connection • October 2003 (Volume 22, Issue 2)

Teacher Files

Maintain a small file box with hanging files for each teacher who frequents the media center. In the file go the teacher's worksheets, your collaboration notes, Internet sites, etc. You can share teachers' ideas with others and you can add other sources you uncover to the file.

Barbara Schiefler, Alvarado Middle School Media Center, Union City, California
Library Media Connection • November/December 2003 (Volume 22, Issue 3)

Lesson Plan Notebooks with Sheet Protectors

To keep lesson plans updated and adaptable, use a large binder with sheet protectors for each grade level. Put each lesson plan in a sheet protector in the grade level appropriate binder. Jot down changes and additional ideas to enhance the lesson; then just add them to the sheet protector pocket with the appropriate lesson plan. In the upper right hand corner of the lesson plan, note the date and grade level(s) that had that lesson. You have an instant, at a glance, way to check if you need to do or have already done the lesson.

Aileen Kirkham, Rosehill Elementary School, Tomball, Texas
Library Media Connection • October 2004 (Volume 23, Issue 2)

Project Binders

When team-teaching a lesson or project with teachers, ask them to suggest a topic. Write up a bibliography and possible project/paper plans for them to use. Refine them together and make notes of what works and what doesn't. Keep copies of the bibliographies, teaching tools, and handouts in a 3-ring binder labeled by year. That way, when the teachers come back frantically the next year and say, "What was that project we did on the Revolution?" you can pull it out. This process is also handy for children who lose their materials. I find filing projects by date rather than by teacher is preferable as units are usually done in the same order each year.

Anne Shipley, Waterloo, New York
Library Talk • September/October 2000 (Volume 13, Issue 4)

Circulating Supplies

Every year, teachers and students come to the St. Joseph Academy Library to borrow scissors, markers, glue, and other production materials for class projects. This year, I decided to capitalize on that need. I purchased four heavy duty plastic bins and stocked them with class sets of scissors, rulers, a paper punch, markers, paper, a stapler, glue sticks, and other supplies. Then I bar coded the bins for easy circulation. I included the cost of the items in my budget, presented a rationale for the purchase, and the administration approved the purchase. The availability of the bins has promoted a lot of goodwill toward the library. In addition, when teachers stop in the library to check out the bins, I never miss an opportunity to talk with teachers about new print and electronic materials that may be useful to them in their teaching.

Leanne Gilgenbach, St. Joseph Academy Library, Cleveland, Ohio
Library Talk • March/April 2001 (Volume 14, Issue 2)

Thematic Map

The library media center is a great place to display a poster-size representation of major themes being taught in the school by each grade level all year long. Ask teachers to e-mail you their major themes or units each month and arrange them in a table or chart visible for other staff, administrators, and parents to see. This "snapshot" curriculum map is also a great timesaving strategy. It enables the library media specialist to stay informed and help teachers by suggesting books and media that may supplement their specific units.

		Oct.	Nov.	Dec.	Jan.	Feb.	March	April	May
1st	Insects & Eric Carle								
2nd	Pond Life & Arnold Lobel								
3rd	Communities								
4th	Wisconsin & Laura Ingalls Wilder								
5th	Colonial Life								

Sue Dohr, Willow Glen Elementary School, St. Francis, Wisconsin
Library Media Connection • February 2005 (Volume 23, Issue 5)

TEACHING
TOGETHER

Coupon Math

To give students pragmatic practice of basic math, distribute several cents-off coupons, with the retail price of the item written on them, to each student. The students can then calculate the:

- final price with savings on each item,
- sum of the savings of all items,
- final cost for all items without savings,
- final cost for all items with savings, and
- percentage saved on the total amount.

Claudette Hegel, Bloomington, Minnesota
Library Media Connection • April/May 2003 (Volume 21, Issue 7)

Cookbook Inspired Reading

Introducing cookbooks and their international recipes is a wonderful way to encourage children to respect and accept multicultural foods. The children can cook (or help cook) and bring samples of favorite foreign recipes to class and share and exchange recipes with classmates.

Madeleine Hoss, Metcalf Laboratory School, Illinois State University, Normal, Illinois
Library Media Connection • November/December 2003 (Volume 22, Issue 3)

Lessons for Kindergarten

Celebrate "Teeny Tiny Day." You can read stories about tiny things on the day you choose. Read *The Teeny Tiny Teacher* by Stephanie Calmenson. Students recognize familiar "teeny tiny things" in the illustrations. Then read *The Teeny Tiny Woman* by Paul Galdone. Children participate in the refrain "Give me my bone." Next, give hints about hidden dollhouse miniatures. Children guess what they are by your description. For example, this is a chocolate and you eat it on your birthday. Then, hold up a miniature chocolate cake. This is planted in your garden. Then hold up a little plant. Describe any object which is "teeny tiny." They love this! Give out a teeny tiny snack such as animal crackers or goldfish crackers.

Gayle Stein, Central Avenue School, Madison, New Jersey
Library Media Connection • November/December 2004 (Volume 23, Issue 3)

A Magnetic Personality

Poetry magnets are intriguing, but the size is small and the cost is large. Whenever you visit a convention, trade show or fair, pick up every free magnet available. Cut the magnets into two or more strips depending on their size. Students or adults can type words (14–20 point size) in columns on a sheet of paper. Laminate the paper or cover each word with wide library tape, trim, and attach with spray adhesive to a magnet strip. Kids like nominating words for the magnets. Metal doorframes, cookie sheets, and teacher desk fronts are good playing fields for the poetry.

Sheryl Kindle Fullner, Nooksack Valley Middle School, Everson, Washington
Library Media Connection • February 2005 (Volume 23, Issue 5)

Celebrate National Poetry Month

We set up a poetry wall in the library that wraps around a bank of circulation computers facing out into the LRC. Students use a colored erasable marker to write an original poem on this cartoon-fringed wall. Initials, first names, or full names are acceptable, but each poem has an identified author. In other locations around the LRC student lockers have "locker" poems that grace the locker doors. Students create an "Ode to My Locker" poem, which is written on a brightly colored sheet the size of their locker and decorated with original art or doodles for the artistically challenged. The culmination of National Poetry Month is a poetry slam entitled "A Night at the Blue Iguana Cafe," which features a café decorated LRC with tropical plants, spotlights, iridescent wall hangings, iguanas (not live!), a jazz quartet, and delicious cafe desserts and beverages. A student club provides both the food and the service while raising money for charitable organizations. The microphone is open to any age poet including parents, students, grandparents, and siblings. This series of events has grown over three years and attracts a large crowd of participants.

Paulette Goodman, Kennedy Junior High School, Lisle, Illinois
Library Media Connection • March 2004 (Volume 22, Issue 6)

Using a Harry Potter Theme

If your students enjoy the Harry Potter books, use a Potter theme to teach sorting. During a solemn ceremony, read the sorting hat song from J. K. Rowling's first book. The children select a piece of colored paper from a wizard's hat. Red for Gryffindor, yellow for Hufflepuff, blue for Ravenclaw, and green for Slytherin. Teachers get short forms to award points of good behavior and academic achievements—just like in Harry Potter books! Students bring the form to the library and place it in a specially marked basket, so it can be tallied at the end of the day. You can make this practice part of a Parents as Reading Partners program where children also receive points for turning in their reading records on time.

Kate Lallier, Robert W. Carbonara School, Valley Stream, New York
Library Talk • November/December 2000 (Volume 13, Issue 5)

Old Globes: New Mars

Most dusty school closets will yield an ancient out-of-date globe. (Old globes are also available at garage sales and thrift stores.) They are not old enough to be collectible, just old enough to be obsolete. We took our plastic globe and had students tear pieces of red, white, and orange tissue paper, which they glued on with decoupage medium. Then the students used the Internet and a NASA atlas to label the dried globe with major Martian features. Now that the two rovers have landed, we are adding those sites. Globes with broken supports can be suspended from the ceiling using clear fishing line.

Sheryl Kindle Fullner, Nooksack Valley Middle School, Everson, Washington
Library Media Connection • March 2005 (Volume 23, Issue 6)

Dictionary Deluxe

Have a dictionary competition for grades four through six. Call out a word and ask a specific question about that word. For example, identify the guidewords for root, or what part of speech is route, or what is the first (or second) definition for route. The child who stands first with the correct answer wins the point. The children with the highest points go on to competition within their grade. We do this once a year; the children look forward to it every time.

Margaret Waites, Perrine Baptist Academy, Miami, Florida
Library Talk • November/December 2001 (Volume 14, Issue 5)

Deaf Awareness Week

Celebrate Deaf Awareness Week in September to expose children to the deaf culture. Even small children can learn to sign "thank you."

Madeleine Hoss, Metcalf Laboratory School, Normal, Illinois
Library Talk • May/June 2001 (Volume 14, Issue 3)

Library-History Correlation

In our eighth grade, each student reads a dozen historical fiction books over the course of the school year. Correlating with each history unit at hand, these books help make history come alive and become memorable to the students. Classroom activities for each book ensure that students will read books in their entirety. Here are some suggested books:

- Salem Witch Trials—*Beyond the Burning Time* by Lasky
- Revolutionary War—*My Brother Sam Is Dead* by Collier
- Voyageur books—*The Broken Blade and Wintering* by Durbin
- Lewis and Clark—*The Journal of Augustus Pelletier* by Lasky and *Seaman* by Karwoski
- Factory Conditions in latter 1800s—*Ashes of Roses* by Auch
- Civil War—*No Man's Land* by Bartoletti (South) and *Soldier's Heart* (North)
- Racism—*Roll of Thunder, Hear My Cry* by Taylor
- Transcontinental Railroad—*Dragon's Gate* (Central Pacific) by Yep and *The Journal of Sean Sullivan* (Union Pacific) by Durbin

Connie Quirk, Mickelson Middle School, Brookings, South Dakota
Library Media Connection • February 2004 (Volume 22, Issue 5)

Encouraging Student Writing and Illustrating

To encourage students to write and illustrate, sponsor an annual Caldecott and Newbery contest. In each class the teacher chooses three selections for the Newbery Award and three for the Caldecott Award from the students' writing-process books. High school English teachers can judge the nominees. One year we had the grandniece of Randolph Caldecott as a judge! Adorn the books with award stickers and give out awards during library media center time, with the winners reading their books to their classmates.

Tammy Sauls, Orangewood Christian School, Mailtland, Florida
Library Media Connection • October 2005 (Volume 24, Issue 2)

Loving Writing

During "I Love to Read and Write Week," we wanted to place more emphasis on writing. The entire staff and student population complete "Writing Hearts" by creating a piece of writing according to the theme provided, decorating the heart, and hanging it in the hallway near the classrooms. Staff members complete hearts and display them together as well. To expand this activity to include community members and families, send hearts home for parents and family members to complete. Last year, we asked parents to write what they love about their children. Students wrote what they love about their parents.

Sarah Davis, Ashland (New Hampshire) Elementary School
Library Media Connection • February 2004 (Volume 22, Issue 5)

Science Is a Shoe In

About once a year we hang clear plastic shoe bags from a tension rod in a library window. Students place items in the pockets that fit our current collection of shells, feathers, seeds/cones, leaves, nuts, or fossils (for safety's sake, no fungi!). Nature books are placed nearby to help students with identification. Students type or write the taxonomy and put it in the pocket with their specimens and their own names. In a leaf collection, younger students might specify "Box elder," while more advanced students would include the Latin "Acernegundo." After four weeks, students vote for the most unusual specimen.

Sheryl Fullner, Nooksack Valley Middle School, Everson, Washington
Library Media Connection • February 2004 (Volume 22, Issue 5)

What Is Today's Equivalent

To teach concepts reinforced by library usage, ask students to copy "new and improved" ads from National Geographic magazine from almost a century ago. They will find things like automobiles, central heat, traveling by ship to Europe, safety razors, coal furnaces—very mundane items—even union suits with only one button! Copy the pictures, and have the children identify what the "new technology" in the ad was supposed to be. Some of them can't imagine that far back, and will need help. Then ask them "What is today's equivalent?" Gives them a good idea that hot technology grows and changes.

Anne Shipley, Waterloo, New York
Library Media Connection • April/May 2004 (Volume 22, Issue 7)

SECTION 5:
USING TECHNOLOGY IN THE LIBRARY

Because of personal computers, networks, the ability to print, school Web sites, and Internet searching, the role of the library media specialist has expanded far beyond the walls of the library media center and of the school. With these new forms of technology have come new responsibilities and new opportunities for school librarians.

Advances in programs for personal computers have led to new applications—programs that offer new ways to aid librarians as they manage; teach; collaborate; promote reading; build positive public relations; and communicate with students, teachers, parents, and the public. Along with these advances has come the need for technology training.

Technology-related tips in this section are divided into these topics:

- Computers
- Printers and Printing
- Web Sites
- Searching the Internet
- Useful Library Applications
- Technology Training

COMPUTERS

"Your Students @ Your Library™" Display

Photos of students and events in your library are wonderful screen savers for the computers in your library. I've used photos of authors presenting in our library, students doing research, and kids working at our jigsaw puzzle table, but the most popular shots are of students having a wild time at after-school events in the library! Just take digital photos and save them to a floppy disk. Take the disk around to each computer and save a different photo as your screen saver on each monitor. Change the photos often!

Laura Stiles, Cedar Valley Middle School, Round Rock ISD, Austin, Texas
Library Media Connection • April/May 2006 (Volume 24, Issue 7)

Dishwasher Safe

For cleaning the "gooky gunk" that accumulates on computer keyboards, made by the use of many fingers, use:

1) Alcohol on Q-tips
2) Windex™ on a paper towel or sponge
3) Baby-wipes
4) The dishwasher! (Definitely for Macs, maybe for PCs).

Cindy Brown, Big Sky and Sentinel High Schools, Missoula, Montana
Library Talk • November/December 2000 (Volume 13, Issue 5)

Computer in Use

I made attractive, laminated signs that read, "computer in use." Students prop these up against the monitor (usually using the keyboard to hold it in place) when they leave the computer to look for a book, indicating that their computer isn't available even if it appears to be. This way, they can continue working at the computer when they return. This is especially helpful with the second graders who are just learning to search the OPAC and find materials on their own in the library.

Laura Mench, Lower School, Lake Ridge Academy, North Ridgeville, Ohio
Library Talk • November/December 2000 (Volume 13, Issue 5)

Computer Signs

Dollar stores sell clear plastic picture frames that have the base built in. They come in a variety of sizes and can be displayed on your computer monitors to tell which programs are loaded at the station, or to give instructions for operating a program, finding the library Web, and other helpful hints.

Pat Miller, Austin Parkway School Library, Sugar Land, Texas
Library Media Connection • March 2004 (Volume 22, Issue 6)

Wallpaper

Scan pictures of student artwork, the student of the month, individualized READ posters, or pictures of student's individual interests and accomplishments and set them as the "wallpaper" on your library computers. Students love to see themselves and their friends displayed on the computer screens. This is a very popular feature of our library and excellent PR.

Suzanne Brown and Cara Russell, Parkview High School Library, Springfield, Missouri
Library Talk • January/February 2000 (Volume 13, Issue 1)

Managing Floppy Disks

If students use library media center floppy disks to save work, a good way to manage the disks is by numbering them. Starting with one, write a large, distinct number on each disk. When handing students disks for saving work, point out the disk's number and tell students that they will need to remember the number to find their work in the future. Having colored floppy disks makes remembering even easier. "I need disk orange five!"

Deb Logan, Taft Middle School, Marion, Ohio
Library Talk • January/February 2001 (Volume 14, Issue 1)

Recycling Disks

Often back-ordered books come with fewer than five MARC records on the disk. After importing and indexing all the records, I move the write-protect tab on the disk from "read only" to "write" mode and use them instead of buying new disks for the library. It is convenient and a form of recycling.

Sheryl Fullner, Nooksack Valley Middle School, Everson, Washington
Library Talk • January/February 2002 (Volume 15, Issue 1)

It's In the Stars

In our library computer lab, we named each computer after a character in the zodiac. Each computer monitor bears a big label with its name (Sagittarius, Libra, Leo, etc.) and is identified on the network by that name. Students who want to use these computers check out a plastic pass, a paddle, matching a given computer. The paddle has a name label and barcode for easy checkout by our circulation system. Students love to ask for computers by name, and librarians can see at a glance that students are using the right computer.

Paul Scaer, J. R. Masterman Lab and Demonstration School,
    Philadelphia, Pennsylvania
Library Talk • January/February 2002 (Volume 15, Issue 1)

Desktop Patterns as Geography Lesson

Instead of the same old desktop patterns, we set the desktop patterns on our lab computers to pictures of different places in the United States and made a monthly contest out of guessing the locations. To start, we kept it simple and used easily identifiable places such as the Grand Canyon, Niagara Falls, the White House, etc. Students fill in the locations on a piece of paper and correct entries are put into a drawing for prizes. This desktop lesson is something fun for the students that could be expanded to other topics (places in the world, animals, famous people, whatever). It could even tie in with a unit of study.

Jane Carlson, Ellis Middle School, Austin, Minnesota
Library Talk • September/October 2002 (Volume 15, Issue 4)

The Multitasking Tip

When working on two programs simultaneously, my favorite speed tip is to use the "Alt" + "Tab" (Mac: "Command" + "Tab") combination to toggle between them. (Note: This is a favorite trick of students to hide a game they're playing by quickly switching to a program they're supposed to be working on.) It's easy to use this trick: Hold down the "Alt" key with your thumb, then press the "Tab" key with your index finger. Then, let go of the "Alt" key. This changes the program you're using to the last program that was accessed. To return to the first program, repeat the process. If you have multiple programs open, continue holding the "Alt" key down while pressing the "Tab" key. Notice that the selection device will toggle through icons representing all programs that are open. Release the "Tab" key at any time to open the selected icon.

Dusti Howell, Emporia (Kansas) State University
Library Media Connection • January 2003 (Volume 21, Issue 4)

PRINTERS
AND PRINTING

Coffee Filters

Simple white coffee filters are versatile and handy in the library. Dampen one slightly with glass cleaner and use it to clean computer monitors. Dampen slightly with water and use to clean laser printers. Remove the toner cartridge and carefully wipe off any rollers inside the printer that may accumulate lint and dust. Use dry filters to clean microscope and digital camera lenses and viewfinders. The coffee filters are so effective because they are lint-free.

Janice Gumerman, Bingham 7th Grade Center, Independence, Missouri
Library Media Connection • February 2005 (Volume 23, Issue 5)

Print Error Screen

Here's a way to swiftly communicate a problem to the local technology person or a software support agency at a distance. Press the control and the print screen keys simultaneously (print screen is usually above and to the right of the regular keyboard) while the error message is still on the screen. Then open a word processing document and press paste. Print out the copy and save for your records, and send the copy via e-mail to the technology person. The tech will be able to see exactly what error message you are receiving without your having to write it all down. The tech also will get other clues about what applications are currently open. When information on resolving the problem is received or discovered, type that into the word document along with the date. Place in a binder titled Tech Log. If the problem is encountered again, flipping through the error messages shows the solution.

Sheryl Fullner, Nooksack Valley Middle School, Everson, Washington
Library Media Connection • February 2004 (Volume 22, Issue 5)

WEB SITES

Star Reviewers

We have a section on our school Web site called Star Student Reviews. Students briefly describe their favorite book. I type their comments and take the student's picture with the book and post it on our site. This has generated a lot of positive response and encouraged reading. (If students don't have written parental permission to have their picture on the Web, I type only the comments.)
http://www.gpisd.org/%7Ejackson//studentrev.htm

Katie Sessler, Jackson Middle School Library, Grand Prairie, Texas
Library Media Connection • April/May 2004 (Volume 22, Issue 7)

URL Address Book

To help us navigate the oceans of information on the Internet, I started a URL address book—in a REAL address book kept on my desk. I included only addresses of "tried and true" best Web sites. The address book will fold back, and many times I just hand the book to the student for them to type in the URL if they are lost in the storm of research. This enables me to work with many students at once. Several of our teachers have said what a great idea they thought the address book was. It certainly helps from year to year to be able to find that "perfect" research site again.

Anna Lee, Swanson Middle School, Arlington, Virginia
Library Media Connection • January 2003 (Volume 21, Issue 4)

SEARCHING
THE INTERNET

Preparing Students for Internet Problems

When getting your students ready to search on the Internet, let them know that you are aware that they could accidentally find themselves on an inappropriate site. Some pornographic sites are set up to thwart the use of the back button. Teach your students to immediately turn off their monitor and get an adult if they ever are uncomfortable with a Web site.

Deb Logan, Taft Middle School, Marion, Ohio
Library Talk • March/April 2001 (Volume 14, Issue 2)

Print AND Online

When you work with a class on a research project, you often suggest helpful Web sites for them to use. Rather than have students write the URLs by hand (and possibly record them incorrectly), give them a custom made bookmark. Students appreciate having something to mark their spot in a book and a quick reference for Internet use during study hall or at home.

Jenni Seibel, D.C. Everest Middle School, Weston, Wisconsin
Library Media Connection • October 2004 (Volume 23, Issue 2)

USEFUL
LIBRARY APPLICATIONS

Market the Library

In order to help market the library and reading, I use the scrolling marquee option for screen savers on our library computers. Every other week or so, I change the message and the colors used. An example of one I used the first week of school is "Pittsburg Panthers READ to SUCCEED!" I also often put these types of messages in the morning announcements.

Ann M. Gray, Pittsburg (New Hampshire) School
Library Talk • January/February 2000 (Volume 13, Issue 1)

Library as Home Page

Make it easy to use your library media center's online resources outside the library media center. Program the class and computer lab computers to open with your library media center home page. If you have Internet Explorer, open your home page. Go to the bar at the top of your screen and click on Tools, then on Internet Options. You will see that the address of your home page is highlighted in Home Page. Click Use Current then OK. When you exit Explorer and return to it, the library media center home page will automatically open. It's good PR for your resources even if students go on to another site.

Pat Miller, Sue Creech Elementary, Katy ISD, Texas
Library Media Connection • April/May 2006 (Volume 24, Issue 7)

Remote Access Services

If you travel to conferences or vacation and you need to access your office computer from the road, try one of the remote access services. "GoToMyPC" is an example. For about $20 for a month of access, you can open your library database as well as any database subscriptions. Anything you can access from your office computer, including PowerPoint and word processing files, can also be accessed from the beach, a convention, a hotel, a seminar, or Internet cafe.

Sheryl Kindle Fullner, Nooksack Valley Middle School, Everson, Washington
Library Media Connection • April/May 2004 (Volume 22, Issue 7)

Easy Scheduling

You keep a deskpad calendar for class scheduling, but you don't memorize it. Why not make scheduling easier by keeping your media center schedule online? If your school Web page doesn't have room, try {myschoolonline.com}, a free Web site where you can set up such a calendar along with other information. You'll be able to go to any available computer and schedule on the spot.

Robert L. Otte, South Christian High School, Grand Rapids, Michigan
Library Talk • November/December 2001 (Volume 14, Issue 5)

AR Lists on the Web

Exporting the books and quizzes from the program to a file is very easy if you have AR Book Guide. The directions can be found in the manual, using "help" in the management program, or calling customer service. What happens after you export the list depends on the software you have for your site.

Karen Brostad, Bennington (Nebraska) Public Schools
Library Media Connection • March 2003 (Volume 21, Issue 6)

AR5 Quiz Lists

To get your AR5 Quiz Lists (Mac version) on your Web page try the following:

> **In AR Management:**
>
> School—Reports
>
> Reading Practice Quizzes
>
> Group: Sort (by author, title, book level...whatever you want) then select all or just the ones you want (If you have a lot of quizzes, you may want to break these into small groups.)
>
> PRINT: a) Change Destination to FILE, b) Change General to "Save as a file"; format should be POSTSCRIPT JOB
>
> Click PRINT, which saves the file. Be sure to keep the ".ps" extension to designate it as a postscript file when changing the name.
>
> Open ADOBE ACROBAT DISTILLER (<www.adobe.com/support/downloads/acdmac.htm>) and a window will appear.
>
> Go to FILE
>
> Click OPEN and select the file(s). It/they will be changed to a PDF with the same name (the extension will be ".pdf").
>
> Add the file(s) to your Web page with a link. Check your Web publishing software for details.

Barb Engvall, John Campbell Elementary School, Selah, Washington
Library Talk • September/October 2000 (Volume 13, Issue 4)

TECHNOLOGY TRAINING

Share and Share Alike

We use the mentor approach to technology training as an efficient way to move everyone on our staff forward. The Technology Committee selects a "topic of the month" to target for instruction. One-third of the staff, who are most proficient in the selected topic, is designated as mentors. They participate in a Thursday morning before-school class led by the staff member who is most proficient in the selected topic. For each of the next two Thursdays, the remaining two-thirds of the staff attend class. Each mentor meets with two mentees from these two groups to complete an assignment. Assignments are always tasks that teachers need to do anyway, and can be accomplished more efficiently through the use of technology.

Sarah Davis, Ashland (New Hampshire) Elementary School
Library Media Connection • February 2005 (Volume 23, Issue 5)

Two Minutes of Technology

Teachers can be reluctant technology users and notoriously leery of change. We break this ice with "Two Minutes of Technology" at every faculty meeting, in which various teachers from different departments demonstrate a technology they're using. These presentations are brief, entertaining, real, and reassuring. On the agenda they're listed as "Brought to You by the Library," which gives us extra credibility, yet the only things we have to do are arrange for the presenters and introduce them.

Kathy Fritts, Jesuit High School, Portland, Oregon
Library Talk • September/October 2002 (Volume 15, Issue 4)

Library MOLE

No time for staff development? MOLE (Mentoring OnLine for Excellence) can provide teachers with an effective tool for utilizing and investigating Web resources that enhance student learning. Initiate a brief e-mail to all teachers. In the e-mail, include one or two URLs for teachers to click on and investigate. Teachers, at a time convenient for them, are then exposed to a variety of sites and resources. Teachers can send a site suggestion back to the MOLE coordinator, who then features it in the MOLE system. Desktop staff development promotes educational objectives, and it is a great motivator for teachers, as technology becomes a tool for discovery.

Terry Zablocki, Boerne (Texas) High School
Library Talk • November/December 2002 (Volume 15, Issue 5)

SECTION 6:

PROMOTING READING

Elementary school librarians promote reading in hundreds of creative ways including storytimes, booktalks, puppet shows, and readers' theater. With displays and bulletin boards and thorough reading incentive programs, the motivating intent is to bring students in contact with books and information. Savvy librarians use student recommendations, plan special events, employ special tactics, and utilize technology to promote reading.

Tips in this section address:

- Storytimes, Booktalks, and More
- Displays and Bulletin Boards
- Reading Incentives
- Student Recommendations
- Special Events
- Special Tactics
- Utilizing Technology

STORYTIMES,
BOOKTALKS, AND MORE

Storytime Treasures

Introduce each storytime by hiding the book and a related prop inside a large decorated box. I use a sewing chest that I painted and covered with glitter and jewels. Cover the book with a shiny cloth, lay the clue on top, and allow students to take a turn weekly. The child shows the clue, and takes three guesses from the audience. Then he/she snaps out the cloth with a "ta-da" and shows the book.

Pat Miller, Austin Parkway School Library, Sugar Land, Texas
Library Media Connection • January 2004 (Volume 22, Issue 4)

Booktalking Bookclub

One way to easily select titles to booktalk is to browse the book club fliers from companies such as Scholastic and Troll. You can booktalk the titles you own that are advertised in the flier. This way, students will learn more than the summary provided in the flier. For students who want to buy books, you'll be helping them make up their minds. For students who don't buy books, you are giving them the option of reading the same books that their classmates may be buying. Either way, you are likely to increase circulation and introduce great titles to students! You'll also be making a connection with the teachers who distribute the fliers.

Laura D'Amato, Lake Ridge Academy, North Ridgeville, Ohio
Library Media Connection • August/September 2003 (Volume 22, Issue 1)

Catchy Lesson Introductions

Storytelling props work for all ages.

When sharing Mother Goose rhymes with my kindergartners, I wear my storytelling apron. Out comes a candlestick for "Jack be nimble," a cardboard pie for "Little Jack Horner," a plastic egg for "Humpty Dumpty," a boot for the "old Woman who lived in her shoe," a clock and a mouse puppet for "Hickory Dickory Dock."

These short poems provide many opportunities to show clues, which help students guess the rhyme.

Read: *Rotten Teeth* by Laura Simms to first and second graders. Introduce it using "Chattering wind-up" teeth. Use a wind-up mouse for *Alexander and the Wind-Up Mouse* by Leo Lionni. Introduce *Lilly's Purple Plastic Purse* by Kevin Henkes with a Lilly doll and plastic purse. Use these props during the story, too. Don't forget the movie star sunglasses and shiny quarters! A blanket is a great lead-in for *Owen* by Kevin Henkes. Hold up a purple pebble for *Sylvester and the Magic Pebble* by William Steig.

Wear "hats." Of course, Dr. Seuss's red and white striped hat is a standard.

Wear a witch hat for *The Witch's Broom* by Chris Van Allsburg. A magician's hat for *Walter's Magic Wand* by Eric Houghton is perfect. Put on a cowboy hat for *Boss of the Plains* by Laurie Carlson and decorate a straw hat with flowers for *Jennie's Hat* by Ezra Jack Keats.

Gayle Stein, Central Avenue School, Madison, New Jersey
Library Media Connection • November/December 2004 (Volume 23, Issue 3)

Booktalks with Visual Aids

Sixth graders love booktalks. To cover as many books as possible in one class period, set up four rectangular tables end-to-end in the front of the library media center. Create a backdrop for the books using a variety of shapes and sizes of empty boxes draped with colorful plastic sheeting. Place your new fiction books to be shared on bookstands at various elevations on the tables. Accompany each with an item representing the storyline. For example, Lasky's Ga'Hoole series can have a stuffed toy owl and an owl call; *The Tale of Despereaux* can have a stuffed mouse with exaggerated felt ears. As you deliver your talk, have a helper parade in front of the watchful students with each book and item. The next day, get your reading teachers to ask the students, as a class, to recall as many of the items as possible in five minutes. Give prizes to the class with the best score. Multiple copies of your new titles will cover demand.

Connie Quirk, G. S. Mickelson Middle School, Brookings, South Dakota
Library Media Connection • February 2006 (Volume 24, Issue 5)

Book Talk Requests

When doing book talks to students, give each student a 3x5 card (I use old catalog cards) and have them put their name and student number on the card. As you talk about books, have them write on the card the title of the book they want to put on reserve. At the end of class, collect the cards. Back at the library, you have the information you need to put books on reserve for them. This process will save students from having to come to the library later to request the book.

Mary Ann Reese, Xenia (Ohio) Central Middle School
Library Media Connection • April/May 2006 (Volume 24, Issue 7)

Scary Booktalks

When asked to booktalk to students, divide mystery/suspense/scary books into two categories as you present: realistic and supernatural. Before you begin the actual talks, lead the class in a discussion of which elements they might expect to find in each category, and continue to discuss which category they think is scarier. This can get rather lively as students have strong divided opinions! (Some of your families may not want their children reading books with supernatural elements, and this method helps those students make informed choices.)

As you show the books, also ask the students why they think there are more girls/women than boys/men on the covers. The response is "because girls get scared easier," to which the girls will vocally protest. Then talk about publishers putting images on the cover that they think will help sell the book. After this, the guys don't seem so shy about picking up a book with a girl on the cover.

When you present booktalks on science fiction and fantasy books, before you begin, go over definitions of the two genre. List elements that they might find in each genre. Discuss books they've read and movies they've recently seen, as this actually adds to the definition of science fiction and fantasy. As you talk about each book or certain authors, categorize fantasy or science fiction. Students have told me they appreciate this way of presentation because it helps them find books they will want to read.

Carol A. Burbridge, Jardine Middle School, Topeka, Kansas
Library Media Connection • October 2005 (Volume 24, Issue 2)

Basic Puppet Collection

To start a puppet collection, visit garage sales and resale shops; have volunteers make them, purchase them, etc. Try to get a variety of farm animals (cats, dogs, chickens, etc.) and have enough to pass out one per child in the group. A simple skit is Old MacDonald Had a Farm. The same group of puppets can adapt to a lesson at a later time on "Old Mac Donald Had a Ranch." The book, *Book! Book! Book!* makes a delightful skit, too.

Aileen Kirkham, Rosehill Elementary School, Tomball, Texas
Library Media Connection • October 2004 (Volume 23, Issue 2)

Readers' Send-Off

Send your graduating students to middle school with a mission to read! Near the end of the school year, carefully select books from your area middle school's library media center. Choose an intriguing collection of fiction and nonfiction books. Include some old favorites that can be found in both libraries. Select some appealing books that are "too old" for your elementary collection. Schedule times to booktalk the books. You'll leave the students anxious to visit their new library media center.

Deb Logan, Taft Middle School, Marion, Ohio
Library Talk • May/June 2001 (Volume 14, Issue 3)

Readers' Theatre Signs

Before doing a Readers' Theatre presentation with a group, I make one "sign" for each character using clip art from the computer. The picture should somehow represent the character. I laminate the signs for durability, punch holes in the top, and then use yarn so the sign can be loosely hung around the student. While Readers' Theatre is usually done with few (or no) props, this enables the audience to remember which character is speaking. This is particularly important when there are several characters. The signs are then stored together with the scripts for future use.

Laura Mench, Lake Ridge Academy, North Ridgeville, Ohio
Library Talk • January/February 2001 (Volume 14, Issue 1)

Puppet Pot

Make a simple stage for your puppets from a large vinyl flowerpot. Cut a hand-sized opening from the side with tin snips or other heavy scissors. Tape the edges of the opening with book tape, set it in your lap, and you can slip your finger or hand puppets in through the back to pop up for a dramatic entrance.

Pat Miller, Austin Parkway School Library, Sugar Land, Texas
Library Media Connection • February 2004 (Volume 22, Issue 5)

DISPLAYS
AND BULLETIN BOARDS

Caught Reading

Prepare a bulletin board entitled "We Are Reading, Too!" to introduce students to faculty and staff. Photograph each staff member and mount the picture along with the name, grade level, or team and a short comment about a book the staff member has recently enjoyed. Students and faculty enjoy looking at the pictures and reading about recommended books. After a couple of weeks, ask students to add their book recommendations, and "Join Us."

Norma Jones, Bessemer City (North Carolina) Middle School
Library Media Connection • February 2003 (Volume 21, Issue 5)

Promoting Reading

To promote literacy throughout your school, establish a permanent "Reading" bulletin board. Ask teachers for a personal photograph taken when they were in middle school, along with the title of a book they enjoyed reading as a teen. Display these "Once upon a time... we read, too" selections during your school's fall open house. Parents and students will enjoy seeing teachers as teen readers!

Barbara Hirsch, Hastings Middle School, Upper Arlington, Ohio
Library Media Connection • January 2006 (Volume 24, Issue 4)

READING
INCENTIVES

Free Reading Incentives

Some FREE incentives for students that you can use with reading incentive programs include:

- First in lunch line pass
- Free homework, tardy, and/or hall pass
- Sit in teacher's chair for one class period
- Create bulletin board for a teacher
- Lunch with a teacher
- Teacher aid for one class period

These incentives proved to be a hit with both the middle school students and the school's pocket book!

Angela Vietti O'Kane, Montieello Trails Middle School, Shawnee, Kansas
Library Media Connection • March 2003 (Volume 21, Issue 6)

Bibliographies for AR Collection

When students come in to select an AR book, they are sometimes overwhelmed by the huge selection, especially in the fiction area. From a jobber's Web site, make a list of AR books as if you were ordering them. (A competent student can do this work.) Then choose an annotated bibliography from their options, and print out copies for each AR teacher. Put the bibliographies in a binder. The students enjoy browsing, and the teachers also have a better idea of what the books are about.

Anitra Gordon, Ypsilanti, Michigan
Library Media Connection • January 2005 (Volume 23, Issue 4)

The Prize Is Reading!

Do you need an inexpensive prize for students who win a class or team game? Allow the winning team to check out an extra book! The kids like the privilege, it promotes reading, and it's free.

Pat Miller, Walker Station Elementary, Sugar Land, Texas
Library Talk • January/February 2001 (Volume 14, Issue 1)

Atomic Champion Reading Success

At our middle school, students can earn reading incentives that are funded by PTA and local businesses. After a basic reading requirement of three books per grading period, students reading an additional book earn Bronze-level status (a fast food coupon), with Silver (school ice cream coupon), Gold (free mini-golf game), Platinum (drawing for mall gift certificate), and Titanium (free aquatic center ticket) for greater numbers. The highest level, Atomic Champion, is for those students who read at least nine books per grading period and pass comprehension quizzes for them. Atomic Champions are invited to the media center for a pizza café lunch served by the school's administrators.

Louise Scott and Betsy Simmons, Creekland Middle School,
    Lawrenceville, Georgia
Library Media Connection • August/September 2004 (Volume 23, Issue 1)

STUDENT RECOMMENDATIONS

Student Approved

I maintain a notebook of simple student reviews in the library media center. For each of the favorable reviews, I fold an index card in half lengthwise and write on the outside: Recommended by student's name. I note the title and call # on the inside of the card for future use. I prop the card on the outside cover of the book on display. It is amazing to see those recommended books fly off the shelves. As an added bonus, students are eager to write more reviews so they can see their recommended book on display. I was able to create a check-in note in our circulation program to alert me when one of the recommended books was returned, so I can easily display it again with its card.

Marcia Krantz, Hudson Falls (New York) Middle School
Library Media Connection • January 2006 (Volume 24, Issue 4)

Librarian Orientation

To get to know both students and the collection when you are new to a building, have the students write down a list of (a) hobbies/interests and (b) what/who they like to read. You can use this information to assess the collection and find some gaps you might fill. You can also incorporate the information into booktalks and lessons. I have asked the teachers to give this as morning "bellwork." They appreciate the suggestion and also like to see what the students write.

Laura D'Amato, Thoreau Park Elementary, Renwood Elementary, Parma, Ohio
Library Media Connection • August/September 2004 (Volume 23, Issue 1)

Book Review File

Keep an index card file box and a supply of index cards available for students to complete mini book reviews. Information on the cards can include title, author, call number, a sentence or two about the book, a rating system (such as a letter grade or number of stars), and the name of the reviewer. File the cards by title or subject.

Claudette Hegel, Bloomington, Minnesota
Library Media Connection • February 2003 (Volume 21, Issue 5)

Reading Favorites

Close to the end of the school year, ask your current middle school sixth graders to fill out a half page form. On it ask students to share in two or three complete sentences their favorite book read in the past school year and why. Categorize the hits into categories: Fantasy, Mystery and Suspense, Real Life Situations, and Sports, typing the titles under the appropriate category. Select a few comments and type these on the back of the reading list but without the students' names. That way it will be the books that are highlighted and not particular students. You can hand out these lists to current sixth graders for summer reading recommendations, and you can give the list to incoming sixth graders next fall as books recommended by their peers.

Connie Quirk, Mickelson Middle School, Brookings, South Dakota
Library Media Connection • February 2005 (Volume 23, Issue 5)

What Should I Read?

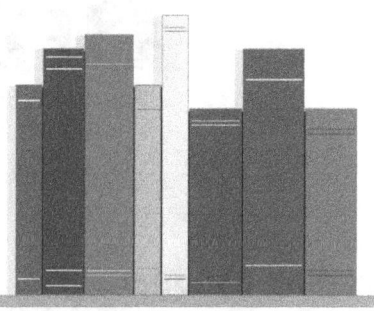

For third through eighth grade students, create a "What Should I Read?" box of book recommendations. After reading a book that is available in your media center, put the bibliographic information, summary, and call number on an index card. Note any awards given to the book, and if a movie was based on the book. File the card in a decorated index card box or recipe box, and place the box in a central location. Students can flip through the cards to find books that are of interest to them. The box is especially helpful when the media specialist is unavailable to make recommendations. You may allow students to place a star sticker or write their own comments on the back of the card after they've read a book. This provides a form of "peer review" in addition to the summary.

Laura D'Amato, Parma (Ohio) City School District
Library Media Connection • January 2005 (Volume 23, Issue 4)

SPECIAL EVENTS

Reading Banquet

Host a Reading Banquet. Each reading class uses the theme of a different book to decorate an eight-foot table with placemats, mint cups, bookmarks, and centerpieces. Arrange the tables, which can include everything from *The Cat in the Hat* to *Charlotte's Web* to *Holes*, in the school gymnasium or other large room. Charge students, families, and community members about $5 to view the tables and attend the banquet. Students can serve generous desserts, prepared by teachers. Other students can provide musical performances, read poetry, or write and perform book skits. It will be a great family night for your school and can raise funds for your library media center. We make ours an annual event!

Bev Gustafson, Lexington (Nebraska) Middle School
Library Media Connection • August/September 2005 (Volume 24, Issue 1)

Book Chat

We participated in "Book Chat in the Library" through the Barnes & Noble booksellers in town. Their qualified representatives exhibited their most current books and discussed the biographies of certain renowned authors. The students were encouraged to discuss, criticize, and give their opinions on the genre of the books they are reading in the classroom or ones they had read earlier. This program included grades 4-8, and the students responded well to this different form of reading encouragement.

Madeleine Hoss, Metcalf Laboratory School, Illinois State University, Normal, Illinois
Library Talk • March/April 2000 (Volume 13, Issue 2)

Library Leprechaun

To celebrate St. Patrick's Day with our kindergarten through second grade students, we read fairy tales from Ireland. After our story time, an imaginary leprechaun visits the library leaving little green footprints all over and a basket of green candy from Ireland for all the students.

Jenny Garrison
Library Talk • March/April 2002 (Volume 15, Issue 2)

Share the Wealth

Preparing for an author or illustrator visit is well worth all the effort necessary, but asking teachers to share a severely limited supply of the visitor's books as they prepare can hamper even the best plans. While it's necessary to buy multiple copies of the author's books in advance, it's also often possible to borrow copies of the books from other schools in the district and even from the public library. A quick temporary cataloging of the items makes it easy to circulate them and retrieve them at the end of the visit.

Toni Buzzeo, Longfellow Elementary School, Portland, Maine
Library Media Connection • April/May 2005 (Volume 23, Issue 7)

Make Author Visits Even More Worthwhile

The presentations of visiting authors are more enjoyable if students have read or heard the author's books. To make a few books go a long way, involve teachers in a drawing. Teachers enter each time they read one of the author's books to their classes. Just before the visit, draw several names. If you have funds, give away autographed books. If funds are tight, take photos of the winners with the author, or invite the winners to a lunch with your special guest.

Pat Miller, Austin Parkway Elementary School, Sugar Land, Texas
Library Talk • January/February 2002 (Volume 15, Issue 1)

Library Camping

Take your kids camping. Begin by pulling all the books you have on camping, both fiction and nonfiction. Then set up small pop-up tents in a circle. You can bring in any camping gear you may have: sleeping bags, flashlights, etc. Ask other teachers to help. Dress in jeans and flannel. Read with the lights out and the flashlights on. Share your favorite book on camping with your kids.

Lisa Fuller, Rock Cut Elementary School, Loves Park, Illinois
Library Talk • May/June 2001 (Volume 14, Issue 3)

Who Was That Masked Reader?

Every morning during our weeklong celebration of reading and writing, Mystery Readers read poems over the intercom. Each class guesses the reader's identity and sends a guess to the office. Winners are announced in the morning notices. We also have two or more readers reading partner poems to make it more of a challenge. There are no prizes: just laughs for some of the incorrect guesses and the satisfaction of being correct.

Sarah Davis, Ashland (New Hampshire) Elementary School
Library Media Connection • March 2005 (Volume 23, Issue 6)

SPECIAL
TACTICS

Reading Mascot

Choose a reading mascot for the year. It can be a giraffe, a frog, a pig, etc. Focus all decorations and activities in the Media Center around the chosen mascot. In January, celebrate Reading Month with contests, art, music, and dance projects. At the end of the month, celebrate the mascot and reading with a Reading Luncheon. Students who complete a contest involving both reading books and a companion project are chosen to attend. Invite the superintendent, the principal and other adults who love children and reading to come and have lunch with the children. Classes "show off" how they have integrated the mascot into all the different curriculum areas.

Bobbi B. Hudson, Woodrow Wilson Magnet School, Danville, Virginia
Library Talk • November/December 2001 (Volume 14, Issue 5)

Caldecott Activity

After looking at possible Caldecott winners for the year, have students write to the illustrator of their favorite book. Attach a student made award to the letter and mail them out. Perhaps some will write back. Even if their book was not a winner, each child has an opportunity to reflect on their choice and a sense of satisfaction at expressing their opinion of their winner.

Lenore Piccoli, Mt. Pleasant Elementary School, Livingston, New Jersey
Library Media Connection • November/December 2003 (Volume 22, Issue 3)

Quick Read

An activity to interest students in new books is what we call a "Quick Read." We put one new title at each chair at the beginning of class. Students look at the jacket, the title, and author and read the book flap information before beginning to read on to page one. They continue reading for seven minutes and then pass the book to the left. Now each student has a new title to follow the same exact procedure until directed to stop and pass to the left again. We have four students at each table, so we do this four times and each student has a chance to become acquainted with four new titles. There is always great demand to check out the books. To maintain fairness, our rule is that the first person at the table to read that title is first to check it out and the others can place holds to be in the queue. We have also used this idea with teachers at faculty meetings to introduce them to new books.

Sue McGown, St. John's Lower School, Houston, Texas
Library Media Connection • January 2004 (Volume 22, Issue 4)

Fantasy Series

Do you struggle to remember the order of the many fantasy series out there? Type up a two-sided handout that contains favorite fantasy authors, with titles listed in series order. Put copies on a rotating stand on the checkout counter. Students like to check off books read and now have many suggestions at their fingertips.

Connie Quirk, G. S. Mickelson Middle School, Brookings, South Dakota
Library Media Connection • February 2006 (Volume 24, Issue 5)

Middle School Lit Requests

Middle school students often request books of a specific type, such as tear-jerkers, humorous books, sports fiction, teen pregnancy fiction, child abuse fiction, fast page turners, etc. It is not always easy to think of a recommendation on the spur of the moment. Keep a three-ring binder with lists related to issues teens ask about. Each time you finish reading a book, add the title and author to one of the lists.

Mavis Schipman, Douglas Middle School Library, Box Elder, South Dakota
Library Media Connection • March 2005 (Volume 24, Issue 6)

Registrar's Gift Books

When new families arrive after the start of the school year, the registrar at our school gives them a new paperback book to welcome them. She said it's been a great ice breaker with parents and reinforces the fact that we encourage reading. I provide these books to give away through bonus points, free books with book fair sales, discounted remainders, and other venues.

Aileen Kirkham, Willow Creek Elementary, Tomball, Texas
Library Media Connection • August/September 2004 (Volume 23, Issue 1)

Using the Daily Newspaper for Reading

In addition to encouraging students to use the daily newspaper as a research tool, I invite them to read the newspaper for pleasure and to learn about different cultures. By reading the newspaper, the children become acquainted with the world and learn about the governments, beliefs, values, languages, holidays, and festivals of various cultures.

Madeleine Hoss, Metcalf Laboratory School, Illinois State University, Normal, Illinois
Library Talk • May/June 2000 (Volume 13, Issue 3)

License Plates

Let your third through fifth grade students make personalized license plates that promote reading. Allow them to use no more than seven letters, numbers, or a combination because that is the rule for real license plates. Some examples include:

> RDGISKL   ILUV2RD   RD2LRN
> KDZREAD   BKSRUL
> RD4LIFE   RD4FUN

Use Print Shop to make a replica of your state's license plate. Use the replica to print the students' plates. Display them in the hall. What a conversation piece!

Madeline L. Buchanan, W. J. Christian School, Birmingham, Alabama
Library Talk • March/April 2000 (Volume 13, Issue 2)

Putting the Chirp in the Cricket

What do you do when your *Very Quiet Cricket* (by Eric Carle) is TOO quiet and chirps no more? The chirper device is made up of a small speaker, circuit board, and two batteries. To remove the chirper, use a sharp thin blade to detach the "anchor," which is two or three pages from the back of the book. Then use the blade to separate the back cover sheet from the back cover cardboard to get out the device. This takes a bit of maneuvering. After the device is out, it can be opened with a VERY small Phillips head screwdriver. Remove and clean or replace the batteries. Clean the circuit board with alcohol. Reverse the procedure to put the chirper back into the book. Then tape the cover sheet and "anchor" back down.

Julia Steger, Clifton Forge Elementary Schools, East and West, Clifton Forge, Virginia
Library Talk • November/December 2001 (Volume 14, Issue 5)

"Share-a-Magazine" Library Corner

To get children reading, invite students to share articles from magazines. Participants can have their names published in the monthly school newsletter.

Madeleine Hoss, Metcalf Laboratory School, Normal, Illinois
Library Talk • January/February 2001 (Volume 14, Issue 1)

UTILIZING TECHNOLOGY

What's New in the Library Media Center?

It is difficult to get information to students on new books, sequels, or just good books to read. At our middle school, we videotape morning announcements and show them during advisory/homeroom each day. One or two times a week we feature "What's New in the Library Media Center." Students read book reviews, list new arrivals or sequels, or feature current displays in the library media center. Students also get a glimpse of what the new books look like. Is it effective? Often the showcased book will be gone before advisory period is over!

Karen Reiber, Nagel Middle School, Cincinnati, Ohio
Library Media Connection • January 2006 (Volume 24, Issue 4)

Recorded Booktalks

Many companies that sell recorded books have sample readings available at the click of a mouse. I turn my computer volume control up to fill the library media center space and then pick a popular new book. The sample chapter rolls out in sonorous or stentorian tones of the professional reader. Students are mesmerized. Some have even missed part of their lunchtime to listen to the readings. This serves as a free booktalk even while I am busy with circulation.

Sheryl Fullner, Nooksack Valley Middle School, Everson, Washington
Library Media Connection • August/September 2005 (Volume 24, Issue 1)

SECTION 7:

BUILDING
POSITIVE PUBLIC
RELATIONS

Savvy school librarians know that their actions are always being observed by teachers and staff, students, parents, and community members. Elementary librarians work to build positive feelings toward the school library media center through personal interaction, thoughtful gestures, special events, bulletin boards, and displays of books and materials.

This section includes:
- Teachers and Staff
- Students
- Parents and Community
- Special Events
- Bulletin Boards and Displays

TEACHERS
AND STAFF

Appreciate Your Patrons

Consider thanking all the people who use your media center by having an appreciation week for teachers, students, or administrators. The week could include serving snacks at an informal social, showcasing the different services your media center offers, and showcasing and previewing library materials. You could offer small tokens of thanks such as bookmarks, pens, water bottles, etc. This is your way of making your patrons feel special and encouraging new patrons to see what the media center is all about. Be sure to advertise this event with bright, colorful flyers or daily announcements, or make a commercial promoting the event during announcements or Channel One time.

Mercedes Smith, Bishop Kenny High School, Jacksonville, Florida
Library Talk • May/June 2002 (Volume 15, Issue 3)

Staff Candy Jar

At the beginning of the school year, announce at a faculty meeting or during staff orientation that the library will have a staff candy jar. Note that the library will fill it the first time, but that donations are requested to keep it filled throughout the year. Be sure to send out donation e-mail reminders when it gets close to being empty and after any holiday when candy is on sale. You may also want to provide a sugar free jar too, for those with dietary constraints. This provides a sweetened respite for your staff on those really tough days and is great PR for TLC from the library.

Aileen Kirkham, Rosehill Elementary School, Tomball, Texas
Library Media Connection • November/December 2004 (Volume 23, Issue 3)

Library Open House

During semester work days, offer a Library Open House for teachers, secretaries, custodians, staff, and administrators. To inform of the event, post flyers by the teacher mailboxes, on the bulletin board, in the weekly newsletter, and put notes in conspicuous places. For the open house, display new books in the library grouped by Dewey category. Provide lots of snacks, finger foods, and candy for treats, and enter everyone for door prizes. Include prizes such as note pads, fancy pens, posters, mouse pads, disk storage boxes, and so on. The door prize slips also document how many people attend.

Janice Gumerman, Bingham Seventh Grade Center, Independence, Missouri
Library Media Connection • January 2004 (Volume 22, Issue 4)

STUDENTS

Question of the Month

Every month I have a QUESTION OF THE MONTH. I post the question (with graphics from Print Shop) in the library and around school. It is also announced on the P.A. system. The question can be categorized as:

- Seasonal—Do vampire bats really suck blood?
- Current Events—Who is the leader of China?
- Related to a Topic a Teacher is Teaching—Match the author to his or her literary works.
- Curiosity—Why do penguins have fur instead of feathers? What causes hiccups? How come neon glows?
- Specific Subject Area—How many different life forms exist on Earth? How far does light travel in a nanosecond?

Students write their name, homeroom number, and answer on a small slip of paper. A winner is drawn at the end of the month by a student in the library for study hall or research. If the first slip drawn has the wrong answer, we keep drawing names until we get a slip with the correct answer. We have only one winner per month. Prizes include nail polish, soap on a rope, a fun pencil, and a gift certificate to a fast food restaurant.

Sue Dwars, Andrean High School, Merrillville, Indiana
Library Talk • March/April 2000 (Volume 13, Issue 2)

You Oughta Be in Pictures

To promote books and technology, use your digital camera to take pictures of students reading a book, newspaper, or magazine during National Library Week in April. After cropping and labeling each picture with "National Library Week" and the date, insert them into mouse pads located by the computers in the library media center. Students love to see themselves in pictures!

Mary N. Stallings, Poquoson (Virginia) High School
Library Talk • March/April 2002 (Volume 15, Issue 2)

Buying Publicity

To get students and faculty excited about an upcoming book fair, distribute gift certificates. The week before the book fair, each child writes his or her name on a slip of paper and adds it to a bucket. At the end of class I draw one name. The student gets a "gift certificate" worth $5.00 that can be used at the book fair. Date the certificates so that a child has to use it the year that he or she wins it. The money used for the gift certificates comes out of profits, but the excitement it brews is worth every penny.

Judy Nicholas, South Highlands Elementary Magnet School, Shreveport, Louisiana
Library Media Connection • January 2005 (Volume 23, Issue 4)

Creative Menus

Our school district uses popular author names in the menus planned during National Library Week (e.g., Peter Rabbit carrot sticks or Alice salad).

I displayed books written by the authors on the menu in the cafeteria. We had trivia questions each day from the books on display. Students received prizes of popular CDs, disks, reading posters, books, money, and ice cream.

Rosa L. James-Alston, Bruton High School, Williamsburg, Virginia
Library Talk • January/February 2001 (Volume 14, Issue 1)

PARENTS
AND COMMUNITY

Getting Parents into the Library

To get more parents to visit the Library Media Center on conference days, post the schedule of events and times inside each door with directions to the Library Media Center; hold registration or refreshments in the Library Media Center; schedule student readings of poetry or creative writing; present Reader's Theatre performed by students; display student-made art or curriculum projects; create new book displays and/or theme centers; hold mini concerts from band, choir, and orchestra; invite teams holding student-led conferences to use your warm and inviting facility. Remember, if their kids are involved, they'll come…sometimes even grandma and Aunt Gertie.

Candace R. Miller, Taft Middle School, Marion, Ohio
Library Media Connection • April/May 2004 (Volume 22, Issue 7)

Literacy Packet

A parent activity that does not involve asking for money can be a literacy packet for parents attending parent/teacher conferences. Put in the packet lists of best books from previous years, a bookmark, a flyer about the state supported information databases, information about public library programs, lists of book reviews, Internet sites for reading, etc. Go around to all of the classes before the conferences and tell the students if their parents came to the library to pick up a packet, the student will get a chance to win a free book from their homeroom. This provides some incentive for the student to encourage the parents to come to the library. Parents can also sign up for best book updates by leaving their email addresses. After the first of the year send them the links for the new best books for the current year. This activity is a quick, easy way to promote the library and meet some of the parents.

Mary Ann Reese, Central Middle School, Xenia, Ohio
Library Media Connection • November/December 2005 (Volume 24, Issue 3)

Books That Shape Lives

For National Book Week, put a letter in the local newspaper and the district newsletter asking community members to send in the names of their favorite childhood books, along with any thoughts about the impact of books on their lives. The information can be sent by mail, e-mail, voice mail, or in writing via a student. Display the responses in the library. Share some of the replies during every library class and feature some of the most eloquent ones on the morning announcements every day during National Book Week. You can also use lists of favorite titles that people mentioned for an OPAC search activity. Your students will be amazed to find that many of people's childhood favorites are still favorites that you have in your library today.

Jan Siebold, Parkdale Elementary School, East Aurora, New York
Library Media Connection • October 2003 (Volume 22, Issue 2)

Author Folder

When hosting an author or illustrator visit, we create an "Author Folder" for each teacher who's involved with the visit. Starting with a twin-pocket portfolio, we paste a color cover illustration from one of the author/illustrator's books on the outside. Then we fill the pockets with an author bio, review clips, activities and information from the author's Web site, a bibliography of his or her books, an order form, and a compilation of curriculum tie-in activities to use in the classroom when reading the author's books.

We also create a family brochure that goes home with each child two weeks before the visit. On colored 8 1/2 x 11 paper, we create a single-fold flyer with an author photo and signature on the front. Inside is a biography of the author, an annotated bibliography of his or her books, and, if space permits, a family activity. The back cover always features a letter from me to families, introducing the author in a more personal way. All illustrations in the brochure are student-drawn.

Toni Buzzeo, Longfellow Elementary School, Portland, Maine
Library Media Connection • January 2003 (Volume 21, Issue 4)

Donor Ideas

Metal and canvas folding chairs often go on sale in September. These are not the old style director's chairs, but ones that are used for camping and sports. They come with their own bags. On open house night, display items such as these canvas lounge chairs that parents can buy for the library. Next to the display put a large envelope with the store's name written prominently on it. The parents put money or a check into the envelope. On the canvas chairs you can ink in the name of the donor with a permanent fine point marker.

Sheryl Fullner, Nooksack Valley Middle School, Everson, Washington
Library Media Connection • November/December 2005 (Volume 24, Issue 3)

Celebrating Black History Month

I invited two mothers to present "Growing Up in the North" and "Growing Up in the South." The children were excited to hear the experiences that the mothers had when they were growing up, and the students' questions were plentiful.

Madeleine Hoss, Metcalf Laboratory School, Normal, Illinois
Library Talk • January/February 2000 (Volume 13, Issue 1)

An Extra Session

When hosting an author or illustrator at your school, consider paying the visitor for one additional session. However, rather than offering this session during the day to a students-and-teachers-only audience, ask the visitor to return in the evening for a family literacy event. Invite your celebrity to share the importance of reading and family stories with your audience of parents and children. Invite students to ask questions they might not have had time for during the daytime visit. Consider having a book sale and signing to accompany the event.

Toni Buzzeo, Longfellow Elementary School, Portland, Maine
Library Media Connection • February 2005 (Volume 23, Issue 5)

National Library Week

We celebrate National Library Week in the month of April by inviting community members to discuss the topic "Books I Enjoyed Most as a Child." The children enjoy meeting the mayor, their county Sheriff, state representative, state attorney, and the Secretary of State.

Madeleine Hoss, Metcalf Laboratory School, Illinois State University, Normal, Illinois
Library Talk • March/April 2000 (Volume 13, Issue 2)

Sibling Sacks

I collaborated with our local community literacy council to create Sibling Sacks for students who have a baby brother or sister born during the school year. The council provides plastic bags imprinted with the council logo (these could be any type of bag). I provide a book appropriate to read to small children, a book that is age-appropriate for the school-aged sibling, a nice bookmark, and pamphlets from the International Reading Association on the importance of reading to and with young children ("Get Ready to Read") for the parents. The student simply brings in a picture of the newborn or the newspaper birth announcement, and I give him or her a Sibling Sack. It has been a big hit!

Julie Stephens, Calhoun (Georgia) Elementary School
Library Media Connection • March 2005 (Volume 23, Issue 6)

SPECIAL EVENTS

Author Visits

We time our annual spring and fall author visits to coincide with our school-wide, PTO-sponsored book fair. This way, the school focuses on books and literacy throughout the week. The week's events end on Thursday evening with a community Book Fair Gala and Author Signing. We move all of the book-fair cases into the gym; set up an extensive, free-goodies food table in the hallway outside (families donate food to the event); and set up a signing room right across the hall, where families can meet the author or buy his or her books and have them autographed. This rich family event generates lots of excitement for literacy.

Toni Buzzeo, Longfellow Elementary School, Portland, Maine
Library Media Connection • January 2003 (Volume 21, Issue 4)

Author Visit Memories

When an author visits, ask the students who have purchased books for signing to let you take a picture of them with the author. If you take these with a digital camera, it is very easy to take the memory stick to a store that makes prints and well worth the inexpensive cost of each picture. Give the individual pictures to the students and encourage them to glue the picture in the book that was purchased. This helps to preserve a lasting memory of this special occasion and is good public relations for the library program.

Janice Gumerman, Bingham Middle School, Independence, Missouri
Library Media Connection • April/May 2006 (Volume 24, Issue 7)

Special "Friends"

We are blessed with an exceptional Friends of the Library student group on our Almondale Elementary School campus. This group is an integral part of all special library activities. Each year, we host three major library events for our students: The American Girl Tea Party, complete with china teacups and saucers; The Matt Christopher Sports Party; and The Library Sleepover. Our students eagerly anticipate these events each year. All library special events are funded by proceeds from Friends of the Library bake sales conducted a the monthly PTC meetings. Hosting these special library events is a great way to get parents involved and participating in the education and enrichment of their children. With an enrollment of more than 800 students, our Friends of the Library group is very much appreciated for their enthusiastic support of the special library activities.

Kelly Lawrence, Almondale Elementary School, Bakersfield, California
Library Talk • November/December 2000 (Volume 13, Issue 5)

Quiz the Board

Does your School Board know what you do? Is your library media center program front-and-center in their minds? If not, consider requesting a designated time (15 minutes) at a school board meeting. Then as a K–12 team, prepare a fabulous PowerPoint presentation about the role of district library media centers in student achievement. Highlight all aspects of your program using digital photos and a multiple-choice assessment format. It can be a quick and enjoyable method for ensuring that all board members are familiar with you, your program, and your contribution to student success!

Toni Buzzeo, Longfellow Elementary School, Portland, Maine
Library Media Connection • March 2005 (Volume 23, Issue 6)

Welcoming an Author

Hosting an author for an overnight visit? Provide him or her with an inexpensive welcome bag or basket that contains some snacks, bottled water, and a magazine or current newspaper. Include your phone number and suggestions for close places to eat if the author will be on his or her own for any meals. Your thoughtfulness will make your out-of-town guest feel at home.

Pat Miller, Austin Parkway School Library, Sugar Land, Texas
Library Media Connection • March 2004 (Volume 22, Issue 6)

School Board Appreciation Month

Our district sets aside the month of January for school board appreciation. To show that the library appreciates them too, we discover some special hobbies/interests of each member. Selecting a book for each member, we put a bookplate inside with this message: "Placed in honor of John Doe for his dedication and work to support the students of XYZ Elementary. January 2004." Then we check it out to that member and send it to him/her via interoffice mail. One school board member requested to personally return his book and to read it to a group of second graders!

Aileen Kirkham, Rosehill Elementary School, Tomball, Texas
Library Media Connection • November/December 2004 (Volume 23, Issue 3)

Author + Book Fair

When planning an author or illustrator visit at your school, consider planning the book fair to coincide with the visit. Plan an evening open house for the book fair and invite your visiting celebrity to attend. The visitor will have a chance to meet with families, sign books, and be a part of your larger community for an evening. Parents appreciate the chance to meet the visitor who has been spending time with their children during the day, and book sales soar!

 Toni Buzzeo, Longfellow Elementary School, Portland, Maine
Library Media Connection • January 2005 (Volume 23, Issue 4)

BULLETIN BOARDS
AND DISPLAYS

PR Posters

Since we all know you can never have enough PR (or time between classes!), I let my sixth grade classes do poster projects to create PR for the titles of our state student book award nominees. Each group of 3-4 took one book, read reviews of it, and designed posters to advertise that title. We then displayed them around the school. A side benefit was increased circulation with our poster designers!

Mary Elizabeth Butcher, Mt. Vernon (Indiana), Junior High School
Library Talk • September/October 2000 (Volume 13, Issue 4)

Bulletin Board PR

If your school has extra bulletin boards in the hallways, cafeteria or gym, you can use those for added PR for the media center. If no extra boards are available, offer to switch periodically with a classroom teacher who would be relieved of the work for a month or two. This is especially important if you have limited bulletin board space within the media center. Post new book or recommended reading lists, highlight media center activities, feature authors, and more. Be sure to include examples (with photos) of how your media program supports the school district's mission and meets state or national standards or guidelines.

Laura D'Amato, Thoreau Park Elementary, Parma (Ohio) City School District
Library Media Connection • April/May 2005 (Volume 23, Issue 7)

SECTION 8:

WORKING WITH HELPERS

Student helpers and volunteers can provide valuable help for the busy elementary school library media specialist. Student library aides, student assistants, and adult volunteers help with clerical and other library-related work. As a bonus, these helpers often provide double help because a frequent by-product of their work is positive public relations!

Tips in this section are divided into two categories:
- Student Helpers
- Volunteers

STUDENT
HELPERS

Staff Badges

Library Aide pins are costly, difficult to pin on, and most of all unhip. We collected lanyards with id pockets from various conferences and designed colorful inserts for our student workers. Easy and cool and free.

Sheryl Fullner, Nooksack Valley Middle School, Everson, Washington
Library Media Connection • March 2005 (Volume 23, Issue 6)

MC Crew

To get student volunteers in the elementary library, involve the upper graders by creating the "MC Crew" (MC = Media Center). Type up a contract listing the responsibilities of the job and ask the student to have his or her homeroom teacher and a parent sign it, along with the student's signature. Each month I choose about four students for the "A.M. Crew." I am surprised who returns the signed contract to me, and I have been pleasantly surprised that all the students have done a great job and ask to come back for an extra month. The activity the students love the most is making deliveries of books, periodicals, videos, and social studies kits to the teachers. The teachers e-mail me their media center requests each day and the MC Crew delivers!

Esther Peck, Wemrock Brook School, Manalapan, New Jersey
Library Media Connection • February 2005 (Volume 23, Issue 5)

Start a Library Club

All of our library assistants are invited to join the Library Club. The Library Club meets once a month during our regular school activity period. Club meetings provide an opportunity for group training as well as friendship among the assistants.

Arlene Kachka, Resurrection High School, Chicago, Illinois
Library Talk • March April 2002 (Volume 15, Issue 2)

Tub Labels

I purchased a shelving unit that has nine bright-blue plastic tubs, which we use to assemble an assortment of books, at a teacher's request, on a particular subject. I label the tubs with bright signs so students can locate them easily. Our student librarians also compiled their favorite reads in one tub.

Ellen Goldfinch, Bishop's College School, Lennoxville, Quebec
Library Talk • March/April 2002 (Volume 15, Issue 2)

Reading Shelves

Reading the shelves is essential to keep the library media center from chaos, but skilled student or parent volunteers for this task are few and far between. Several times a year, I print out my shelf list after sorting according to call number. It is a job that takes less than five minutes (the printing takes longer of course). Then student clerks or other volunteers, working in pairs, can easily make the shelves match the shelf-order sheet. This eliminates the need to train.

Sheryl Fullner, Nooksack Valley Middle School, Everson, Washington
Library Media Connection • October 2005 (Volume 24, Issue 2)

VOLUNTEERS

Training Volunteers

To help parent volunteers, I type up instruction sheets for our most common tasks: creating and applying a spine label, stamping or putting labels on media, covering book jackets with mylar. These instruction sheets include a list of needed materials and tools, step-by-step instructions, and a sample of the finished product. The sheets are then laminated or slipped into a clear plastic sleeve. All of the sheets have one bold face statement at the bottom: "Grateful for your help in providing library materials that are tidy and uniform." The sheets have minimized my training time for each volunteer.

Sheryl Kindle Fullner, Nooksack Valley Middle School, Everson, Washington
Library Media Connection • April/May 2004 (Volume 22, Issue 7)

Personalized Holiday Gifts for Parent Volunteers

In November, call the children of your parent volunteers in to the library and take each child's photo with a digital camera. Ask the children to write down a special memory or tradition that their family takes part in during their holiday season. Once you have their words and photo, put the two together in a narrow column format—about the size of a bookmark—print each one with color ink, and have each one laminated. As a final touch, punch a hole in the top and tie a ribbon through the hole. Your parent volunteers will be touched by what their children write, and the final product can be used as a bookmark or a holiday ornament.

Laura Stiles, Cedar Valley Middle School, Austin, Texas
Library Media Connection • November/December 2005 (Volume 24, Issue 3)

Stay at Home Volunteers

In the first school newsletter I put coupons that ask for parent volunteers to cover books at home. The coupons ask for the parent name, phone number, student name and teacher. The coupon also asks if the parent needs a video to help them learn to cover books. My clerk and I made a video on how to cover books. When I need some paperbacks covered, I call the parent or leave a message saying I will be sending books home, laminate material, a video (if they need it) in a canvas bag with their child that day. I then check the books out to an account I call "Book Covering" and put a note on it with the parent's name. If the parent has not returned the books in two weeks, the system generates an overdue. I can then call the parent to see if they need more time or ask the child about the progress that is being made. I often will put in age appropriate books for the children of the parents, in hopes that they will read the books before returning them.

Mary Louise Sanchez, Thornton, Colorado
Library Media Connection • March 2006 (Volume 24, Issue 6)

Aroma Bookmarkers

Many magazines have fragrance samples. Volunteers can easily trim off the magazine pages and put the samples in a bookmark bin at the checkout desk. Some magazines have as many as four per issue. We mark each with a male or female symbol; once it is cut from the ad, it may be hard to visually distinguish. This process actually makes the magazines more accessible to allergen-sensitive students without overly perfuming the books into which they are placed. These bookmarks are very popular with our students.

Sheryl Kindle Fullner, Nooksack Valley Middle School, Everson, Washington
Library Media Connection • January 2005 (Volume 23, Issue 4)

Fast Reading Level

There are many online sites that publish reading levels; however, I often run across a book not listed. I quickly type a paragraph into a Word document and hit spell check. At the end of spell check, the Flesch-Kincaid Reading level appears. This process takes less than a minute and can also be done by student or parent helpers.

Sheryl Kindle Fullner, Nooksack Valley Middle School, Everson, Washington
Library Media Connection • January 2006 (Volume 24, Issue 4)

Volunteer Appreciation Day Gift Books

Each year during Valentine's week, we have our Volunteers' Appreciation Luncheon. When the volunteers sign in, they receive a paperback book for their family. I make sure that we have English and Spanish titles since we have eight classes of bilingual students. The front office funds the book purchase, but I select the titles and the vendor.

Aileen Kirkham, Willow Creek Elementary, Tomball, Texas
Library Media Connection • August/September 2004 (Volume 23, Issue 1)

SECTION 9:
MANAGING TIPS FOR THE LIBRARIAN

In the hectic hustle and bustle of the day-to-day operation of the school library media program, it is sometimes easy for the media specialist to get caught up in the daily routine and to neglect personal well being. Never forget that the most important component of the library program is you! Your health and happiness are essential to a workable library. Take time to be healthy. Leave the library occasionally to attend conferences. Read professional books like this one to hone your skills. Pat yourself on the back for the work you do, the most important job in the world!

Library Fitness

As librarians, we have access to more health information than anyone in our nation, yet many of us are sedentary. A great New Year's resolution is to be more active. When walking in school hallways, pick up the pace, and swing your arms. Instead of sending student helpers on long distance errands, let them mind the desk and take the trek yourself. I have used a pedometer to map our school with a goal of walking 2 miles in the course of the workday. My improved efficiency and energy levels more than make up for the brief amount of time I am away from the circ or reference desk.

 Sheryl Fullner, Nooksack Valley Middle School, Everson, Washington
Library Media Connection • November/December 2005 (Volume 24, Issue 3)

Solution to Author Autograph Dilemma

You have an opportunity to get one or two books autographed. What do you do? Do you have the school's copies autographed, knowing that they might be lost or chewed up the first time they are checked out? Do you get your personal copies autographed, knowing that they will be treasured—but feeling bad that your students will not have access to them? Compromise by having your personal copies autographed to you and your students: To Mrs. Logan and her library friends... Share the autograph, how you got it, and stories about the author with your students for many years to come.

Deb Logan, Taft Middle School, Marion, Ohio
Library Talk • March/April 2001 (Volume 14, Issue 2)

Short and Sweet

If you sometimes receive phone calls (such as tech or automation support) that can't be interrupted, print out a variety of short, polite messages in bold fonts on bright paper and laminate them. Attach these to ping-pong paddles (which can be purchased at garage sales) or to large paint sticks. Drill a hole in the handle of the paddle or stick, thread with string or a leather thong, and hang near the phone for instant courtesy. Then, when you're in the middle of a call that you can't interrupt, you can grab a paddle and wave it at your would-be interruption like a virtuous picket sign. Best accompanied by a smile.

Sheryl Fullner, Nooksack Valley Middle School, Everson, Washington
Library Talk • September/October 2001 (Volume 14, Issue 4)

Wrists at Risk

Repetitive stress injuries are no laughing matter, and librarians are among the susceptible. Although we're usually really well informed because data is at our fingertips, those same fingertips may be tingling, numb and increasingly clumsy without proper preventive measures. At **http://www.aaos.org/wordhtml/press/exerci.htm**, you'll find six easy-to-learn exercises that you can do right at the checkout desk. If students ask what you're doing, teach them the moves, and let them know that they could be only one job away from similar damage. Not all learning in the library comes from media! Be a good example of proper wrist care.

Sheryl Kindle Fullner, Nooksack Valley Middle School, Everson, Washington
Library Talk • September/October 2002 (Volume 15, Issue 4)

Freebie Fun

Collect all the freebies that you get from various jobbers throughout the year. Some companies send things such as calculators, radios, or CD players when you buy a certain amount of merchandise. Often Book Fairs award free softcover books to the library media specialists as a promotional device. Use these freebies to give out as contest prizes throughout the year. Students appreciate the special recognition and the cool prizes.

Ann M. G. Gray, Pittsburg (New Hampshire) School
Library Media Connection • February 2006 (Volume 24, Issue 5)

Managing Usernames, Passwords, and ID numbers

How does one keep track of all the usernames, passwords, and ID numbers for various on-line sources? Keep an address book by the computer. The best is one large enough, with plenty of lines for each addressee, to enter several items of information (URL, username, password, phone number for tech support, etc.). I prefer a 5-1/2" x 8-1/2" size. Enter information alphabetically by the name of the Web site for the resource. Keep one at school and one at home. In your home address book you can enter sensitive information (banking, etc.) by code name to avoid problems. The address book is very portable, so you can take it with you when you travel!

Sharon Gonzalez, Connell Middle School, San Antonio, Texas
Library Talk • November/December 2002 (Volume 15, Issue 5)

ABOUT THE EDITOR

Sherry York is a retired school librarian married to a retired school librarian. She and her spouse worked in school libraries and classrooms for more than thirty years before retirement. During their years as librarians, they collaborated on many library- and technology-related projects and shared numerous tips.

Since retirement Sherry has worked as a reviewer, conference presenter, indexer, and Linworth project editor. She has written reviews, articles, author profiles, and bibliographies for *Library Talk, The Book Report,* and *Library Media Connection.* She continues to review for *LMC* and for *VOYA (Voice of Youth Advocates).*

She is the author of four Linworth books:
- *Ethnic Book Awards: A Directory of Multicultural Literature for Young Readers* (2005)
- *Children's and Young Adult Literature by Native Americans: A Guide for Librarians, Teachers, Parents, and Students* (2003)
- *Children's and Young Adult Literature by Latino Writers: A Guide for Librarians, Teachers, Parents, and Students* (2002)
- *Picture Books by Latino Writers: A Guide for Librarians, Teachers, Parents, and Students* (2002).

Sherry and Donnie live on an island in Texas. He manages a reading room while she maintains a flexible schedule. In recent years she has been a judge for the Publishers Marketing Association and for the WILLA (Women Writing the West) awards. She reads mysteries indiscriminately and utilizes technology to expand her lengthy to-read list. In their home, their shelves are not in order and their book collection needs weeding!

TIPS
OF YOUR OWN

TIPS
OF YOUR OWN

www.ingramcontent.com/pod-product-compliance
Lightning Source LLC
Chambersburg PA
CBHW070642300426
44111CB00013B/2220